THE THESSALONIAN ROAD

SANCTIFICATION MADE PLAIN

GARY S. MAXEY

SANCTIFICATION MADE PLAIN

The Thessalonian Road: Sanctification Made Plain

Published by

WATS PUBLICATIONS

West Africa Theological Seminary
36 Olukunle Akinola Street,
Ipaja, Lagos, NIGERIA

Contact Addresses:
Gary S. Maxey, Founder, WATS, PMB 003, Ipaja, Lagos
36 Olukunle Akinola Street
Akinyele/WATS Bus Stop, Ipaja, Lagos, Nigeria.
www.watspublications.com, sales@watspublications.com
ISBN: 9798666332757

Contact Addresses:
Gary S. Maxey, Founder, WATS, PMB 003, Ipaja, Lagos
Email: drgarymaxey@gmail.com; Tel: +234-808-726-6310

Designed and printed by
asbotgraphics
22, Adifashe Street, Ladi-lark, Bariga, Lagos.
+234-803-367-1112 | asbotgraphics@yahoo.com

Table of Contents

Introduction

Sanctification is making or being made holy. Holiness (or sanctity) is the peculiar and distinctive characteristic of God and of all that is specifically associated with God.

The ancient Israelites and the Christian Church are both referred to as "holy nation" (Ex. 19:6; 1 Pet. 2:9). We refer to the Christian Church as an assembly of "saints" not because they are holy by themselves but because of the sanctifying power of God through His word, the blood of Jesus Christ and the Holy Spirit.

Our supreme standard and pattern of holiness is Jesus Christ, the Holy One of God (Mark 1:24; Acts 3:14). God intends his people to be conformed to the image of His Son (Rom. 3:29). This is not fully accomplished within the first moments of our Christian existence, nor is it something we can achieve of ourselves. Sanctification is the work of God's grace, brought about by the Holy Spirit.

So, in his letter to the Thessalonians, Paul eulogised them for their initial acceptance of the word of God through faith (1Thess. 1:1-10), but he equally reminded them that they should not rest on their oars. They should be consistent, persistent and resilient in the midst of temptations that would surely come as a result of their faith in our Lord Jesus Christ.

The Thessalonians and all of us today should strive for peace with all men with holiness, apart from which no one will see God (Heb. 12:14).

Furthermore, God wants all people to be saved and to come to the full knowledge of Jesus Christ His only begotten Son; but not all will heed this call. Some will definitely be dangling between two opinions. However, those who are faithful till the end will be saved.

It is also instructive to note that when one is saved, he is not insulated from sins and double mindedness. So many entanglements will emerge to distract him from the path of God. So, he must strip off every weight that slows him down especially any sin that so easily trips us up; and run with endurance the race God set before us (Heb. 12:1).

We can also note that while Jesus was without sin, yet he was not allowed any respite by the devil right from the temptation in the wilderness (Luke 4:1-13) to the prayer at Gethsemane (Luke 22:41). Christ's aim was to abide by God's will; not his own will.

The process of sanctification that God has marked out for all of us can be summarized thus:

Step I: Initial Sanctification which is the starting point (2 Cor. 5:1; Gal. 5:24).

Step II: Progressive Sanctification (John 17:17).

Step III: Continuous Sanctification comes whenever we feel remorse for sin committed and confess the same (1 John 1: 8,9).

Step IV: Entire Sanctification or Perfection (2 Tim. 4:7,8).

Starting the Christian faith well is important, and it is good. But finishing well should be our ultimate aim.

So, my dear people of God, as we read through this masterpiece by Gary S. Maxey, we should note that holiness is not an option but is compulsory and mandatory. Be prepared to be born again (John 3:5); study the word of God to guide you in the path of holiness (Ps. 109: 11; 1 Pet. 2: 1-2); allow Christ to increase while you decrease (John 3:30); and be filled with the Holy Spirit so that you walk by him (Gal. 5:16). Finally, be aglow in the Holy Spirit (Rom. 12:11).

Holiness which comes from the sanctification by the Holy Spirit is the only sure way to heaven. It is like the compulsory documents for your international travel: Passport and Visa.

I therefore heartily recommend that every Christian must read this "Spiritual Tonic and Cafeteria" by Gary S. Maxey. Be blessed and lifted as you read.

His Eminence, Samuel C. K. Uche
Prelate, Methodist Church Nigeria

Preface

For fifty years I have preached sermons based on holiness texts from 1 and 2 Thessalonians. Paul's prayer in 1 Thessalonians 5:23 is the New Testament verse to which I have most often referred, reflecting my conviction about the deeper work of sanctification that I believe is the birthright of every born-again believer. Perhaps it was inevitable that sooner or later I would write a book on what I am calling the *Thessalonian Road*.

I know many of my readers have not heard of the Thessalonian Road. The much more familiar New Testament "road" is the Roman Road to salvation. The Roman Road has gained popularity as a way of explaining the good news of salvation, using verses from the Book of Romans. It starts with Romans 3:23, showing the need for salvation ("for all have sinned and fall short of the glory of God"). It then progresses to Romans 6:23, which talks about the consequences of sin ("For the wages of sin is death, but the gift of God is eternal life in Christ Jesus"). Romans 5:8 shows us God's solution, through the death of Jesus Christ ("But God demonstrates his own love for us, in that while we were still sinners, Christ died for us"). Romans 10:9 then explains the need to confess Jesus as Lord and to put our faith in him ("If you confess with your mouth that Jesus is Lord and believe in your heart that God raised him from the dead, you will be saved"). The road ends with Romans 5:1, which shows the result of salvation, which is peace with God ("Therefore, since we have been declared righteous by faith, we have peace with God through our Lord Jesus Christ"). The Roman Road has been effectively used hundreds of thousands or perhaps even millions of times both in personal evangelism and also from the pulpit.

The idea of a Thessalonian Road, to deeper sanctification, is a parallel concept. It is not original with me, though frankly I cannot remember how and when I first heard it described. Yet it has been clear to me for a long time that 1 Thessalonians gives one of the clearest, and somewhat biographical, expositions in the New Testament of the need for a deeper work of sanctification in the life of believers. As I have noted, I have been preaching about this road for a long time, though not every time explicitly using the road metaphor. I am pleased finally to share it with a wider audience in book-form.

I am candid to note that I am not writing this book because I believe my own Christian experience is a flawless model. Far from it. I have shared in my spiritual autobiography that going on to an experience and life of deeper sanctification, after I first came to Christ as a teenager, was something that utterly and forever changed my life for the better. I believe in holiness of heart and life, and I see this Thessalonian Road as an extremely important matter. I have not followed the road flawlessly, but I thank God that I am on the Highway of Holiness today, with anticipation of a great hereafter.

Unless otherwise noted, all scripture quotations in this book are from the NET Bible (New English Translation). I warmly acknowledge the encouragement and editorial contributions of my long-time friend and brother, Ralph Tilley, whose own writings and teaching on sanctification are noteworthy.

Over the past years I have enjoyed the continuing support of many others around me in my teaching, preaching and writing ministries. Spending our senior years in Africa is one of the best decisions Emma Lou and I have ever made. As this book goes out, we both pray that God will make it a great blessing to as many as possible. To God be the glory!

Dr. Gary S. Maxey
West Africa Theological Seminary
15 November 2018

> **Unlike many today, Paul did not see holiness as one *option* for ministry focus. Today we like to think of it in that way: Church A focuses on deliverance; Church B focuses on discipleship;...while Church E preaches holiness as their own emphasis. That is not what is reflected in the New Testament, and certainly not in the life, ministry and writing of Paul. Rather, he saw holiness as an essential part of his message**

HOLINESS AND THE MISSIONARY MINISTRY OF PAUL

No New Testament writer has been more thoroughly examined and understudied than the apostle Paul. He towers above other New Testament writers, like Kilimanjaro over the Tanzania plain. He is the greatest theologian in the history of Christianity. He speaks to us through thirteen epistles, containing a total of eighty-seven chapters. His pen spills forth words at once fatherly and assuring, yet elsewhere stern and even angry, and, yet again, pleading and weeping. What was written scores of generations ago, still speaks loud and clear today, with a contemporary relevance that at times astounds us.

What was the driving force behind this great man? What sent him for twenty or more missionary years, over countless robber-infested and rugged miles of hills and valleys and unpredictable seas? What enabled him to rise again and again from beatings, famines, robberies and shipwrecks to continue his journey? What was it that enabled him to say with satisfaction toward the end, "I have fought a good fight" (2 Tim. 4:7)? What, after all, was that good fight all about? Is there anything that we could rightly label the key that most effectively opens his teaching to us?

THE FORCE OF PAUL'S CALLING

One thing crystal-clear about Paul is that he had a divine call. It forcefully grabbed him and would not let him go. His dramatic conversion and call on the road to Damascus unleashed a force that he never escaped and that colored everything that happened to him thereafter. He was quite clearly driven by an unquenchable fire of divine appointment. He had a vision from God that would allow him no rest until it was fully accomplished.

Paul's call was a multi-faceted one, though it was never muddled. First, he knew that above everything else he was called to proclaim Jesus Christ as the universal and resurrected Messiah. Paul's theology is thoroughly Christ-centered. Paul believed and taught that Jesus of Nazareth was the Son of God sent down to earth in human flesh, in order to reconcile all mankind to God through his suffering, his death and his resurrection. Paul met the glorified Jesus Christ on that Damascus road. He knew not only that Jesus was the Messiah, but also that he was very much alive and sitting at the right of God the Father on high.

Though Paul was a highly educated Jew trained in all the wisdom of First-Century Judaism, there was another component to his theology that was crucial for his calling.

Paul believed Jesus was the fulfillment of Old Testament prophecies and that he had established a New Covenant replacing that of Moses. The clear implication, Paul believed, was that First-Century Christians were no longer bound by ceremonial and dietary laws and by rites such as circumcision required in the Law of Moses. In short, Paul knew it was not necessary to become a Jew in order to be a Christian. That may be common sense to us, but we should remember that in Paul's day it was fresh revelation. As he wrote in 1 Timothy 2:4, God "wants all people to be saved and to come to a knowledge of the truth." Paul was called to proclaim a universal gospel in a way that had not yet been imagined by others.

APOSTLE TO THE GENTILES

A second facet to Paul's unique calling is that he knew he was called primarily to declare the gospel of Jesus Christ to Gentiles. He was born and raised as a Jew. He was not only a Jew, but also a fanatical one (a "Hebrew of the Hebrews," as he put it [Phil. 3:5]). At the point of his conversion to Christianity, nearly 100% of the followers of Jesus were Jewish. There was nothing in his background that would have suggested he would one day be the Apostle to the Gentiles. Yet from the moment Paul was thrown to the ground and almost forcibly recruited by Jesus himself to become a proclaimer of God's truth, Luke tells us his call to the Gentiles was clear.

Almost immediately after Paul's conversion, when God spoke to a hesitant Christian believer in Damascus by the name of Ananias, asking him to receive the bewildered and blinded new convert, Luke tells us,

> But the Lord said to him, "Go, because this man is *my chosen instrument to carry my name before Gentiles* and kings and the people of Israel." (Acts 9:15).

Years later, Paul testified that his call to the Gentiles was reiterated again within a few days after his conversion. As he testified,

> When I returned to Jerusalem and was praying in the temple, I fell into a trance and saw the Lord saying to me, … 'Go, because *I will you far away to the Gentiles.*'" (Acts 22:17-21).

During his first missionary journey with Barnabas, it is clear that though their primary contacts were with fellow Jews they were beginning to focus also on Gentiles, as we see in Luke's report about what happened at Pisidian Antioch in southern Galatia.

> So Paul stood up, gestured with his hand and said, "Men of Israel, *and you Gentiles* who fear God, listen" (Acts 13:16).

Later, when Jewish listeners became jealous and started to resist the gospel message, both Paul and Barnabas took their stand for their mission to the Gentiles.

> Both Paul and Barnabas replied courageously, "It was necessary to speak the word of God to you first. Since you reject it and do not consider yourselves worthy of

eternal life, *we are turning to the Gentiles.* For this is what the Lord has commanded us: '*I have appointed you to be a light for the Gentiles, to bring salvation to the ends of the earth.*'" (Acts 13:46-47)

There can be no doubt that Paul's primary focus throughout the remainder of his ministry was on reaching out to Gentiles with the message of salvation through Jesus Christ. He wrote to the Ephesians, "To me – less than the least of all the saints – this grace was given, to proclaim *to the Gentiles* the unfathomable riches of Christ" (Eph. 3:8). Without Paul's groundbreaking work as the Apostle to the Gentiles, coupled with the cooperation of his fellow Jewish leaders in the Early Church, the story of the spread of Christianity would have been remarkably different.

It is easy for us to see why Paul was uniquely and providentially positioned to serve as a bridge between the Jewish and Gentile communities in the First-Century Mediterranean world. On one hand, he was not only a Jew, but by his own testimony he was a "Pharisee and the son of a Pharisee" (Acts 23:6). He was a Hebrew of the Hebrews, of the tribe of Benjamin (Phil. 3:4-5). He had studied under the famous Jewish teacher, Gamaliel (Acts 22:3), and had advanced in the Jewish religion beyond many others (Gal. 1:14).

At the same time, though, Paul was also a Greek by culture, with a solid Greek education (Acts 17:28; Tit. 1:12), demonstrating familiarity with Greek culture and thinking. He was also a Roman citizen by birth, which is what led him to his appeal to Caesar, starting from when he was imprisoned at Philippi (Acts 16:37-39). We can easily understand why Paul could say, "I am become all things to all men, that I may by all means save some" (1 Cor. 9:22). Nobody in the New Testament was better qualified than Paul to be the Apostle to the Gentiles.

PAUL'S MESSAGE

However, it would be unfair and incomplete to summarize Paul's mission merely in terms of his burden for Gentile conversion. Even in his mission summary in Ephesians 3:8, we can see that his focus is not merely on Gentiles but on preaching the "unsearchable riches of Christ." What did he mean by that? What are those "unsearchable riches"? How did Paul understand the core of his appointed message?

A passage in his letter to the Colossians is a good key to our understanding on this point. Here Paul tells us his primary assignment was "to present every man perfect in Christ Jesus" (Col. 1:28). A look at the larger passage is helpful:

> I now rejoice in my sufferings for you, and fill up in my flesh what is lacking in the afflictions of Christ, for the sake of His body, which is the church, of which I became a minister according to the stewardship from God which was given to me for you, to fulfill the word of God, the mystery which has been hidden from ages and from generations, but now has been revealed to His saints. To them God willed to make known what are the riches of the glory

of this mystery among the Gentiles: which is Christ in you, the hope of glory. Him we preach, warning every man and teaching every man in all wisdom, that we may present every man perfect in Christ Jesus. To this *end* I also labor, striving according to His working which works in me mightily. (Col. 1:24-29)

What does Paul mean by "presenting every man perfect" in Christ Jesus? To be candid, most of us are uncomfortable with the word "perfect," even though it is used frequently not only in the writings of Paul but also by other New Testament writers a total of twenty-five times. Yet in our own day we tend to not like the word. It makes us uncomfortable. We find it easy to say, "But of course I'm not perfect." I believe that makes it all the more important that we ask what Paul meant by his use of this word. After all, he is describing it as a core part of his ministry mission – not just to preach to Gentiles but also to present every man perfect in Christ.

Let me note first that akin to the word "perfect" are similar words in Paul's writings, such as "holy" and "blameless." He writes to the Ephesians that God "chose us in Christ before the foundation of the world that we may be holy and unblemished in his sight in love" (Eph. 1:4). Paul also insisted that as believers we no longer continue sinful living. According to him, believers are "free from sin." He says this loudly and clearly and repeatedly in places like Romans 6.

Are we to remain in sin so that grace may increase? Absolutely not! How can we who died to sin still live

> in it? . . . We know that our old man was crucified with him so that the body of sin would no longer dominate us, so that we would no longer be enslaved to sin. (For someone who has died has been freed from sin.) . . . Shall we sin because we are not under law but under grace? Absolutely not! . . . having been freed from sin, you became enslaved to righteousness. (Rom. 6:1-2, 6-7, 15, 18)

Paul clearly took these matters seriously. He believed the gospel of Jesus Christ was not mere window-dressing for people who in reality remained enslaved to their old life and old habits. He believed life in Christ was not about stumbling through life in a state of perpetual struggle and repeated defeat from the sinful nature. He also practiced what he preached. He talked to the Thessalonians, for example, about his own blameless walk before God and his expectation that they, too, would emulate that kind of living:

> You are witnesses, and so is God, as to how holy and righteous and blameless our conduct was toward you who believe. As you know, we treated each one of you as a father treats his own children, exhorting and encouraging you and insisting that you live in a way worthy of God who calls you to his own kingdom and his glory (1 Thes. 2: 10-12).

A PASSION FOR HOLINESS

What we are discovering here is that at the core of Paul's missionary calling was his passion for holiness. Paul was a *holiness man* through and through. Unlike many today, Paul did not see holiness as one *option* for ministry focus. Today we like to think of it in that way: Church A focuses on deliverance; Church B focuses on discipleship; Church C focuses on evangelism; Church D specializes in signs and wonders; while Church E preaches holiness as their own emphasis. That is not what is reflected in the New Testament, and certainly not in the life, ministry and writing of Paul. Rather, he saw holiness as an essential part of his message, closely related to and explaining everything else.

That brings me back to his use of the word "perfect." Paul's mission was to present every woman and man "perfect" (*telos*, in the original Greek) in Christ. In using this word, Paul refers to his conviction that the entire purpose of the plan of salvation through the sacrificial death of Jesus Christ was to make all women and men exactly what God created them to be. The word *telos* does not relate to our modern sense of Godlike superhuman achievement, but rather to the fulfillment of God's purpose for us. In its root meaning it refers to something that is "hitting the target." Perfection in the Bible sense is to be all God created us to be. Not flawless, but blameless. Not divine or angelic, but "perfect" as God intended us to be. It means simply being what we are designed to be.

God showed us the "target" in both the Old Testament and the New Testament. He told the children of Israel, "Speak to the whole congregation of the Israelites and tell them, 'You must be holy because I, the Lord your God, am holy'"

(Lev. 19:2). God's "target" for all of us is holiness. We are to be holy. Again, not divine or angelic, but "holy" as God intends us to be. Not flawless, but blameless.

Paul strongly believed and taught this concept of holiness everywhere he went. He was convinced that right from the first moment of our surrender to Christ as he experienced himself on the road to Damascus we enter God's great Highway of Holiness. We become God's "holy ones." Paul's two favorite words for addressing his Christian converts were "brethren" (brothers and sisters), and "saints." He used the former word about 100 times in his letters, and the latter more than 40 times. The word "saints" literally means "holy ones." To be a believer, Paul believed, was to be a holy woman or a holy man.

Paul believed the readers of his letters were "saints," and that is why he addressed them as such. They were saints because they were sanctified which is another cherished word for Paul. To "sanctify" means simply "to make holy." Sanctified people have been made holy. All believers are saints, Paul believed, so all of them have been sanctified. They have experienced sanctification. Paul spoke to the Ephesian leaders in Acts 20:32, "And now I entrust you to God and to the message of his grace. This message is able to build you up and give you an inheritance among all those who are sanctified." A bit earlier he had written to the Corinthians, "to the church of God that is in Corinth, to those who are sanctified in Christ Jesus, and called to be saints" (1 Cor. 1:2).

Yet even while calling his converts saints, he also knew they were on a journey that was not yet complete, and that required them to mature or to grow up. They needed to experience a deeper sanctification than they had ever known before.

That is why, as we shall see in coming chapters, in 1 Thessalonians he keeps bringing them back not just to the issues about which they have written to him (primarily questions regarding end-times) but also to their need to go on to maturity in their Christian walk and to experience the deeper sanctification that would enable them to persevere faithfully to the end and to be found blameless at the coming of the Lord.

PAUL'S UNDERSTANDING OF SANCTIFICATION

To understand Paul clearly, we must remember that in his letters he uses the concept of holiness and sanctification in more than one sense. When we fail to appreciate the sense in which he is using it in a particular passage, it can lead to confusion. However, it should not be too difficult to discern what Paul is saying in any given context.

We must first remember that Paul uses the word "sanctification" in its moral sense, and almost never in its ceremonial sense. In the Bible, (especially in the Old Testament) the verb "sanctify" can be used in the ceremonial sense of "setting apart" or consecrating worship paraphernalia or even of people for sacred use in worship. The instruments of the tabernacle and temple were thus sanctified, as were also Aaron the high priest and others serving in worship (Ex. 30:29-30).

In its moral sense, on the other hand, sanctification refers to ethical or moral purity, godlikeness, or holiness. Therefore, to define sanctification as "setting apart" captures only one sense of its Bible meaning, and not even the sense in which Paul normally uses it. When Paul talks about "holy" people, he means people who have been made Christlike in character, through the grace of God.

We must note also that Paul uses this moral sense of sanctification in several different ways. For example, Paul sometimes uses the word "sanctification" in the broad sense of the entire work of God in the life of believers, right from the time of conversion until entry into the gates of heaven. That is the sense Paul invokes in 2 Thessalonians 2:13.

> But we ought to thank God always for you, brothers and sisters loved by the Lord, because God chose you from the beginning for salvation through sanctification by the Spirit and faith in the truth.

Paul uses the word "salvation" here in the broad sense of the rescue of believers from the doom and penalty of sin to eternal life in Jesus Christ. This salvation is brought about "through sanctification by the Spirit and faith in the truth." Remember that "sanctification" means simply "being made holy," or "the act or process of being made holy." So Paul is saying God has chosen to save us by making us holy, through the power of the Holy Spirit and by faith. Salvation means deliverance from the guilt and power and dominion of sin in a process that makes us like our heavenly Father. It is a lifelong process. This is sanctification in the broadest sense, starting the moment we are awakened to new life in Christ and continuing until we enter heaven's gates.

This broad sense of sanctification is normally understood as progressive. Paul is keenly aware of the reality of spiritual progress, spiritual growth, or spiritual maturity that comes about through our daily walk of obedience to God. It is echoed in 1 Corinthians 1:30, where Paul refers to "Christ Jesus, who became for us wisdom from God, and righteousness and *sanctification* and redemption." It is also the sense used by the writer to the Hebrews when he says, "Pursue peace with everyone, and *holiness*, for without it no one will see the Lord" (Heb. 12:14).

Paul at times also uses the word "sanctification" in a more restricted sense, to refer to what happens at the moment of our new birth. Some have referred to this as "initial" sanctification. It is the "washing of regeneration" Paul mentions in 1 Corinthians 6. Paul had already noted in 1 Corinthians 1:2 that he was writing to the Corinthians as "those who are sanctified in Christ Jesus, and called to be saints." He acknowledges that they are already properly classified as "sanctified," or God's "holy ones," even though we see later evidence in his letter that they were not spiritually mature people and indeed were harboring a lot of unChristlikeness in their lives.

In 1 Corinthians 6:11, after Paul described the wicked deeds of unbelievers, he said: "Some of you once lived this way. But *you were washed, you were sanctified*, you were justified in the name of the Lord Jesus Christ and by the

Spirit of our God." He acknowledges that at the point of conversion, when they entered into new life in Christ, they experienced sanctification. They became God's holy people. He is not talking about the broad sense of sanctification mentioned in 2 Corinthians 2:13, but the more narrow sense of initial sanctification received at our new birth. It is similar to the "washing of the new birth" to which Paul refers in Titus 3:5, and very possibly what James is talking about in James 4:8a where he says, "Cleanse your hands, you sinners" (James 4:8). In every case it is referring to a cleansing or purifying work of sanctification at the moment of the new birth.

Finally, in Chapter 5, Paul uses the word "sanctification" in yet another sense. 1 Thessalonians 5:23 is the climax of his appeal to the Thessalonians. He voices a heart-felt prayer to God that they would experience what we can simply call a "deeper sanctification," or what he calls "whole" or "complete" or "entire" sanctification. He says, "Now may the God of peace himself *make you completely holy* and may your spirit and soul and body be kept entirely blameless at the coming of our Lord Jesus Christ." This is surely the same thing Paul refers to in 2 Corinthians 7:1, when he appeals to his readers, "Therefore, since we have these promises, dear friends, let us cleanse ourselves from everything that could defile the body and the spirit, and thus accomplish holiness out of reverence for God."

To deny that Paul sees sanctification as of extreme importance in the life of believers is to miss what should be quite obvious. It was at the foundation of his primary concern for these great Thessalonians believers. But before we turn to his specific words to them, chapter-by-chapter, we need to ask some background questions about these new believers and the times and environment in which they lived. That is the subject of our next chapter.

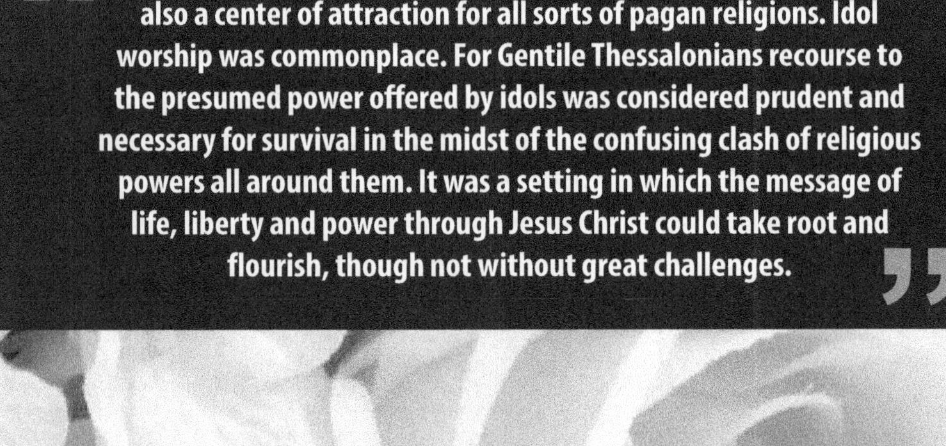

First-Century Thessalonica had a large Jewish population, but it was also a center of attraction for all sorts of pagan religions. Idol worship was commonplace. For Gentile Thessalonians recourse to the presumed power offered by idols was considered prudent and necessary for survival in the midst of the confusing clash of religious powers all around them. It was a setting in which the message of life, liberty and power through Jesus Christ could take root and flourish, though not without great challenges.

WHO WERE THE THESSALONIANS?

THE THESSALONIANS – TODAY AND YESTERDAY

Thessaloniki is the second most populous city in modern-day Greece, after the capital city of Athens. With over 1 million people in its metropolitan outreach, it is home to a diverse population. It is the cultural capital of Greece and also the focal point of the Greek diaspora.

Thessaloniki was founded in 315 BC. It was named after the princess Thessalonike of Macedon, the half sister of Alexander the Great, one of history's greatest military commanders. Because of its strategic location with good access to both land and sea routes, it is not surprising this city was a coveted prize for conquering armies, all the way from the Romans to the Byzantines (who considered it the second city in their empire, after Constantinople) to the Muslim Ottomans to the Twentieth-Century German

Nazis. With its great wealth, its rich culture, and its trade and industrial capacity, we should not be surprised that Thessaloniki was so attractive.

For many centuries, Thessaloniki was home to a large Jewish population. That was certainly true at the time of Paul's interaction with the Thessalonian believers in the First Century. Through the centuries, the Jewish population proved adaptable to the changing political landscape. As recently as 130 years ago, more than one-half of Thessalonian residents were Jewish, according to official Ottoman government census takers. It had become known among Jews as the "Jerusalem of the Balkans," or the "mother of Israel." However, one of the great tragedies of modern times is that under the dominance of Nazi Germany during World War II, tens of thousands of Thessalonian Jews were rounded up like sheep and shipped northward to concentration campus where they were murdered in cold blood. The result is, that in our own day the Jewish population of Thessaloniki has fallen to far less than one percent.

Today, Thessaloniki remains a popular tourist destination. *National Geographic* touts it as one of the top global tourist destinations. Thanks to the spread of global Christianity, and the fact that the Bible is the most widely distributed book in history, for worldwide Christians Thessaloniki is best known as the home of a small Christian congregation, to which the apostle Paul wrote two letters during the time of the Roman Empire.

At the time of Paul's first visit to Thessalonica (as we New

Testament people normally call it) it was a city not of one million inhabitants but less than 50,000. Paul ministered in what today is known as the Upper City. Because of its strategic location and importance within the Roman Empire, this was an ideal place for Paul to minister to both Jews and Gentiles.

THE MORAL AND CULTURAL SETTING OF THESSALONICA

As one of the more prosperous inter-cultural cities within the First-Century Roman Empire Thessalonica during Paul's day was not unlike modern multi-cultural African cities such as Lagos. As a popular crossroad city on trade routes connecting larger centers like Rome and Byzantium, it attracted people from multiple native languages and numerous religious backgrounds. We know from archeological findings that Roman cities such as Thessalonica were centers of gambling, fighting and sexual immorality that even today often comes with geographic and social displacement. As we will see, we have hints of what that meant for the early Thessalonian Christian believers through Paul's comments in 1 Thessalonians 4.

First-Century Thessalonica had a large Jewish population, but it was also a center of attraction for all sorts of pagan religions. Idol worship was commonplace. For Gentile Thessalonians recourse to the presumed power offered by idols was considered prudent and necessary for survival in the midst of the confusing clash of religious powers all around them. It was a setting in which the message of life, liberty and power through Jesus Christ could take root and flourish, though not without great challenges.

The attraction of the gospel was not only potent for Jews who had compromised their faith in God or who were clinging to dead legalism, but also to Gentiles who were aware that their faith in the worship of idols had not proven adequate. Acts 17 gives us a glimpse into the setting that Paul encountered in Thessalonica and other nearby cities. Paul started his evangelism efforts in the Jewish synagogue where, according to Luke, "some of them were persuaded and joined Paul and Silas, along with a large group of God-fearing Greeks and quite a few prominent women" (Acts 17:4). However, the relative orderliness broke down when Paul and Silas were ushered out of the protection of the synagogue. "But the Jews became jealous, and gathering together some worthless men from the rabble in the marketplace, they formed a mob and set the city in an uproar" (v. 5). We get a picture of the challenge of disseminating Christianity in the midst of an idolatrous, immoral and uncivil surrounding world.

THE THESSALONIANS IN THE CONTEXT OF PAUL'S JOURNEYS

While all of Paul's missionary journeys were successful, it appears that his second missionary journey was the most fruitful. He set out from Syrian Antioch with Silas. Eventually they picked up Timothy and Luke along the way, and reached the eastern coast of the Aegean Sea, guided by the Holy Spirit (Acts 16:6-7). They were in a small town in what today is the country of Turkey. There Paul received a night vision in which he was confronted by a Macedonian man calling for him to sail west, cross the sea and come to the aid of Macedonia. Then and now, Thessalonica was the governmental seat of the province of Macedonia. As Paul recounted later in his testimony to King Agrippa, he was not disobedient to the vision (Acts 26:19).

The result was that Paul established two churches in the province of Macedonia: Philippi and Thessalonica. In both cases, serious opposition and danger accompanied his efforts. There were hostile forces, both within Judaism and also among Gentiles, which were opposed to the teachings and practices of this new faith in Jesus Christ as Messiah. In Philippi, the opposition came from Gentiles who were stirred into riotous action against Paul and his companions, following Paul's casting out of an evil spirit (Acts 16). Paul and Silas were arrested, severely beaten and thrown into an inner cell in the city jail. At midnight, as they sang together, a God-timed earthquake shook them loose. Through Paul's witness the jailer, along with his entire family, was converted to Christ. However, after the dust settled, Paul and Silas accepted the appeals of the city officials to quickly leave town. That eventually led to their visit to Thessalonica.

In Thessalonica, Paul and his team proclaimed Jesus as Messiah, starting among some of the Jewish population. Some of them accepted their preaching and joined them, as did a large number of Gentile proselytes, including a good number of prominent women (Acts 17:4). Yet here again, as in Philippi, they eventually ran into serious opposition. After a few short weeks, Paul and Silas were advised to leave town and set off for Berea.

Were it not for what we can now read in 1 and 2 Thessalonians, we might assume that Paul's success in Thessalonica was quite limited, because of the brevity of his time in the city. His visit certainly was short, and it was cut off prematurely because of opposition to his preaching. Yet we know now that Paul had started something that was to have positive nurture and growth for many years to come.

THE THESSALONIANS IN THE CONTEXT OF PAUL'S WRITINGS

Bible scholars do not agree on the exact order in which Paul's letters were written, but it seems clear to most that 1 Thessalonians was one of the first. His letter to the Galatians was probably his first epistle that we have, as evidenced by comparing Acts 16:6,23; 18:23 and Galatians 6:17. If that is true, it is likely that 1 Thessalonians was his second epistle. He wrote it toward the middle of his second missionary journey, some months after he left Thessalonica. While spending a few months in Corinth (in 50 or 51 AD), Paul wrote back to the new believers at Thessalonica. Through this letter we get clear insights into Paul's pastoral heart, and especially the kind of advice he passed on to relatively new believers.

The Pauline Epistles are the thirteen letters written by Paul that are included in the New Testament canon the list of authorized books accepted by the Early Church as of clear apostolic authority. These thirteen letters contain the bedrock of theology upon which Christianity is built, and most especially in relationship to the doctrine of salvation. In Paul's writings we see this salvation expounded in terms of redemption, justification, regeneration, reconciliation and sanctification. At the same time, Paul also talks about issues such as Christology (the deity and humanity of Christ), election, spiritual gifts, church leadership, the relationship between law and grace and future judgment.

There are some who have erroneously suggested that Paul teaches his own brand of Christianity that is not completely in agreement with what Jesus taught or what can be found in the Gospels. This is false teaching. We believe in the Holy Spirit's inspiration, and in the inerrancy and unity of the Bible. All scripture is God-breathed (2 Tim. 3:16). Paul's letters are a part of inspired scripture. Therefore, his teachings are in God-superintended harmony with every other book of the Bible.

Paul's thirteen epistles are divided into two categories: nine of them written to churches (Romans through 2 Thessalonians), and four that are pastoral or personal (1 and 2 Timothy, Titus and Philemon). In his letters to local churches, Paul generally deals with three issues. Of first importance is Christian doctrine. Paul is keenly concerned that new believers he is evangelizing imbibe sound teaching, and especially because of the tendency for false teachers to crowd in and cause confusion. Second, Paul is concerned that his converts apply sound teaching by putting it into appropriate living and actions. Third, Paul always includes instructions and personal greetings that relate to each church with which he is communicating.

Thankfully, Paul's teachings on doctrine and practical application are general enough that they have had universal relevance over the centuries, as multiplied hundreds of millions have read his letters. Husbands are to love their wives, no matter in which culture or age they might live. Children are to obey their parents (Eph. 6:1). Overseers are to be kind to their workers (Col. 4:1).

Paul's letters to the Thessalonians follow the general characteristics I have mentioned. However, they are also unique among his epistles in two regards. The first is that there is more discussion in these two letters about end times and the Second Coming of Christ than in any other of Paul's writings. The reason is that Paul is responding to the expressed concerns of these new Thessalonians believers. They are worried because some of their members have passed away and they are not sure what will happen to them at the return of Christ. Will they miss their opportunity to be caught up in the air to meet Jesus? These and other questions prompt Paul to give sound teaching about end times.

Especially Paul's first letter to the Thessalonians is also unique among his epistles, in going to greater lengths to urge them to *go on* or to "increase more and more" (1 Thes. 4:10 NKJV). He urges them forward to a deeper sanctification than they had known before. He is urging them to travel what in this book I call the Thessalonian Road.

Like all of Paul's letters, his correspondence to the Thessalonians is rich in theology. There is relatively little narrative, as we find elsewhere in the New Testament, especially in the Gospels and Acts. Today we still have the privilege to sit at Paul's feet and learn what it means to be travelers on this great road.

"What is unmistakably clear is that the conversion of the Thessalonians was genuine and was not simply a momentary event with no subsequent progress. Rather, it was followed up by robust spiritual growth. They not only turned from their former idol worshiping, but they began to systematically demonstrate the true fruits of the Holy Spirit.

1 THESSALONIANS 1: A RADICAL TURN TO CHRIST

On our journey through Paul's first letter to the Thessalonians, our eyes are especially open to one issue: Paul's concern for the spiritual welfare and spiritual triumph of the new Thessalonian believers. While Paul was quite solicitous of their questions about end times, he nevertheless kept foremost in his mind and ministry to them the deeper issue of their spiritual wellbeing. Paul knew that questions of eschatology, including the timing of the Lord's return, the order of end-time events, and the fate of various groups involved, are not in and of themselves core spiritual matters. He knew that the ultimate question is our relationship with God and how therefore we will navigate end times so as to end on the winning side.

Even today, that is what should be the top concern of every child of God. Our primary question should not be the timing of Jesus' Second Coming. Rather, Will I be prepared to meet him in the clouds in the air? Or, as some might express it, will I be "rapturable"? Why? Because, as Paul said,

> For the Lord Himself will descend from heaven with a shout, with the voice of an archangel, and with the trumpet of God. And the dead in Christ will rise first. Then we who are alive *and* remain shall be caught up together with them in the clouds to meet the Lord in the air. And thus we shall always be with the Lord. Therefore comfort one another with these words. (1 Thes. 4:16-18)

PUTTING FIRST THINGS FIRST

The primary lesson of Chapter One of 1 Thessalonians is that our journey of faith, which is a journey on God's highway of holiness, must begin with a crystal clear conversion. It is unthinkable to attain a life of holiness without absolute clarity in our initial salvation. To be God's holy people we must first and foremost be born again.

In these first ten verses, Paul begins his letter by rejoicing with the Thessalonians about their new life in Christ. He speaks like a proud parent, which is exactly what he is. In the second chapter, he refers to himself as a *mother* to these believers ("Like a nursing mother caring for her own children, with such affection for you we were happy to share with you not only the gospel of God but also our own lives, because you had become dear to us" [1 Thes. 2:7-8]). Interestingly, in verse 11 he also refers to himself as a *father*, this time saying, "we treated each one of you as a father treats his own children." Later, writing to the Corinthians, he expressed similar parental love, referring to himself again as a *father* ("my dear children. . . . I became your father in Christ Jesus through the gospel" [1 Cor. 4:14-15]). All of these expressions tell us a lot about Paul's genuine love for those to whom he was preaching and later discipling. His love was unmistakable and his pride was undisguised. He bursts out in 1 Thessalonians 2:20, "For you are our glory and joy!"

It is clear in this first chapter, that Paul is proud of the spiritual conversion and spiritual life of the Thessalonians. Unlike some of his other letters (Galatians and 1 Corinthians are the most obvious), this letter contains no parental scolding or reprimands. Rather, it brims over with appreciation, thanksgiving and joy.

There was a sound reason for this, too. As we shall see below, Paul did have a heavy burden for these people and a deep concern about their spiritual progress. Yet he knew it was absolutely important to *put first things first*. The first thing of importance in the life of every human being should be our eternal salvation through Jesus Christ. There is no more fundamental question to ask anyone than, Are you a born-again child of God, and do you know that with certainty? Without a sound answer to that question nothing else matters by comparison.

Jesus said it succinctly to Nicodemus: "You must be born from above" (John 3:7). It is all well and good to talk about believers having this or that experience after their conversion (whether we may call it deeper sanctification or baptism with the Holy Spirit or whatever else), but unless there is absolute soundness in our conversion experience it will all eventually turn to confusion.

THE GENUINENESS OF THEIR CONVERSION

The clear testimony of Christian conversion that we see in 1 Thessalonians 1:1-10 is unparalleled anywhere else in the Bible. Paul gives a multifaceted testimony of the genuineness of their transformation from darkness to light, through the power of Christ. The major highlights are easy to spot:

Verse 5 says, "Our gospel did not come to you merely in words, but in power and in the Holy Spirit and with deep conviction." Paul knew the reason the Thessalonians had experienced genuine conversion was that he had preached the word of God faithfully among them, anointed by the Holy Spirit. The result was that it had produced deep conviction for sin. It is quite similar to what Paul witnessed later among the Corinthians, who like the Thessalonians turned to God from idol worship to become true believers. Paul said of the Corinthians, "you became sorrowful as God intended . . . Godly sorrow brings repentance that leads to salvation and leaves no regret, but worldly sorrow brings death. See what this godly sorrow has produced in you: what earnestness, what eagerness to clear yourselves, what indignation, what alarm, what longing, what concern, what readiness to see justice done" (2 Cor. 7:9-11).

One of the greatest needs in our modern churches is a return to sound line-upon-line preaching of the fundamentals of the gospel. The African Church has a long history of sound gospel preaching, but it must be revived and perpetuated in our own generation. Yesterday's preaching will not suffice for today. Messages must be continually heard about conviction for sin, repentance, confession, restitution, new birth, etc. Those messages must go forth in the power of the Holy Spirit and in such a way that they result in deep conviction for sin. That is exactly what Paul says happened in the case of these Thessalonians.

Verse 9 says, "You turned to God from idols to serve the living and true God." Deep conviction of sin was followed not just by regret or sorrow but also by a total life-transformation. He is talking about a complete turnaround. It was a 180-degree life-transformation, from darkness to light, from idol worship to Jesus worship, and from sin to righteousness and holiness. Bible conversion is far more than mental persuasion. It is radical transformation of life.

When people experience this kind of transformation it is impossible to hide it from others. The transformation is evident for everyone to see. This is why there has always been a sharp and readily observable distinction between those who are truly born again and those who are not. A great turnaround has taken place. As Paul said to the Corinthians, "what is old has passed away," and the new has come (2 Cor. 5:17).

Verse 3 says, "We recall in the presence of our God and Father your work of faith and labor of love and endurance of hope in our Lord Jesus Christ." It should be more than clear by now that Paul is giving an unparalleled testimony of people genuinely born again, who had left their old lives of sinful living behind them and who were brimming over with new life in Christ. No wonder he was a proud parent!

Verse 6 says, "You became imitators of us and of the Lord." Paul knew that a primary mark of true conversion is the forsaking of our old way of life, followed by a radically new life, pursuing after God and after godly people around us. People who have received new life in Christ are automatically attracted to others who are eagerly following God and they begin to imitate them in many different ways.

Verse 7 says, "You became an example to all the believers in Macedonia and in Achaia." Here is evidence that these Thessalonians were not just believers, but model believers about whom Paul could boast. People looking on from outside could see what real Christianity was all about.

Verse 8 says, "From you the message of the Lord has echoed forth not just in Macedonia and Achaia, but in every place reports of your faith in God have spread." When genuine conversion takes place, it is impossible to suppress it and difficult to keep quiet about it. The psalmist writes, "Let those delivered by the Lord speak out" (Psalm 107:2). The Thessalonians are a great example in that regard. Why would the apostle not be proud of such people?

What is unmistakably clear is that the conversion of the Thessalonians was genuine and was not simply a momentary event with no subsequent progress. Rather, it was followed up by robust spiritual growth. They not only turned from their former idol worshiping, but they began to systematically demonstrate the true fruits of the Holy Spirit. Genuine new birth was followed by genuine discipleship and serious spiritual growth.

SAMSON'S SHORN LOCKS

One of the concerns I have over the contemporary Church is that here and there we seem to be gradually losing clear testimonies of salvation, such as we see here in 1 Thessalonians. As a result, I fear that some of our churches are beginning to fill up with people who do not bear the genuine marks of conversion that we can see here. I fear that bold testimonies to the kind of clear New Testament new birth we see with the Thessalonians are becoming progressively rare in too many of our own churches. Instead, we see growing examples where we are creating a mass of followers, yet many of whom have only a vague concept of personal salvation. We have become like Samson with shorn locks.

For one thing, we too often seem unwilling to face the reality of the spiritual lostness and peril of men and women without Christ. We are not gripped as we were in by-gone days by a deep conviction that without a clear personal relationship with Jesus Christ people are inevitably headed toward an eternity without hope and without God. We have forgotten that Jesus cannot heal someone who is not even aware that he or she is sick. We have lost much of our ability to preach against the popular sins of our day and to call a spade a spade. Therefore, fewer people than ever in our churches are gripped with a stinging sense of their spiritual lostness and need.

It is not so much that we have forgotten everything about salvation, but that we have watered down and emasculated our message and our soteriology to the point where we no longer have a clear salvation message that mirrors the teachings of the Bible. We may have retained much of the vocabulary of new birth, but in too many cases it has become divorced from the kind of radical change that is understood within the scriptures. Instead, we have adapted and adopted substitutes that are suitable only to people without a stomach for the truth of the Bible.

It is to be feared that in too many cases we have lost our ability to boldly preach against sin. We seem reluctant to remind our hearers that the penalty for sin is eternity in a place of burning torment prepared by God for the devil and his angels. When we remind people that they will some day face the judgment of God they become uncomfortable or even angry. As a result, we sometimes end up saying quite weakly, "All you have to do is believe in Jesus," or "Make a decision for Jesus," or "Just invite Jesus into your heart."

I fear that in many places we are bypassing the message of radical New Testament repentance. The result is that we run the risk of gradually filling our churches with unrepentant members who claim to be "saved," and who even use born-again vocabulary, but who go on sinning as if there is no judgment day coming and no tomorrow about which to be concerned. By contrast, as we have seen, Paul said of these great Thessalonians that they had "turned to God from idols to serve the living and true God." They had experienced a 180-degree turnaround in their lives. They knew what it was to repent.

The picture is often quite different today. Michael L. Brown, in his book, *How Saved are We?* says this:

> We say, "Just confess Jesus as Lord and you're in!"
>
> He says, "Not everyone who says to Me, 'Lord, Lord,' will enter the kingdom of heaven, but only he who does the will of My Father in heaven" (Matt. 7:21).
>
> We say, "Just pray this prayer and it's done!"
>
> He says, "If anyone would come after Me, he must deny himself and take up his cross daily and follow Me" (Luke 9:23).
>
> We say, "Just come to the altar. It will only take a minute!"
>
> He says, "Make every effort to enter through the narrow door, because many I tell you, will try to enter and will not be able to" (Luke 13:24).[1]

---

[1] Michael L. Brown, *The Rude Awakening, How Saved are We? Has the Church Fallen Asleep in the Enemy's Lap?* (Shippensburg, PA: Destiny Image Publishers, Inc, 1990), 2.

WEAK CONCEPTS OF SALVATION

I thank God that for the most part the contemporary African Church has taken seriously the responsibility for strong evangelism and for clear calls to personal salvation. My first strong impression of the African Church nearly forty years ago was of a Church caught up with an exciting and dynamic passion for evangelism. It was at an exciting level that I had never seen in my native country, and it was clearly driven by the power of the Holy Spirit. It was a passion that compelled men and women into the streets, onto buses and taxis, and into homes and offices to urge others to turn to Christ for salvation. Right from my first days in Africa I could see that the African Church had much to teach the global Church about evangelism. Even today I thank God that the passion for evangelism is still alive and well in many of our African churches.

Gospel-preaching and evangelizing African churches have received and perpetuated the practice of the "altar call" from western revivalism. Over the decades it has been used effectively. Yet I believe we need to examine both our evangelism and our contemporary altar calls to ensure that we do not lose the cutting edge of our effectiveness.

I must be candid to note that the "morning cry" that I heard nearly every day in the 1980s has almost entirely vanished, at least from the neighborhoods I frequent. In its place these days I see a myriad of modern misconceptions about the new birth. Consider the following false or weak concepts of salvation that have become increasingly popular in some of our churches:

<u>Salvation as mere mental assent</u>. This is the increasingly popular idea that salvation is not about repentance, including the possibility of literally shedding tears, or remorse over our rebellion against God. Rather, it has been boiled down to making a mental decision to "accept Christ," or to "believe in Jesus." Some have rightly labeled it "easy believism." It is the idea that one needs only to believe in Jesus in order to be saved and that there is no need for conviction of sin or sorrow for sin followed by a transformed life of committed discipleship. This sort of message is particularly popular today among those who are following the errors of hyper-grace teaching.[2]

Let me be clear here. It is quite true that the scripture says, "Believe in the Lord Jesus Christ and you will be saved" (Acts 16:31). We are correct to believe in the historic Christian teaching of *sola fide* ("faith alone"). But we must also believe that true faith in Jesus Christ will always lead to a changed life, and that faith without works is dead (James 2:17). We are saved by faith alone, but such faith can only arise from a heart that is humbled before God and that is repentant and willing to forsake sin.

Our shallow teaching of salvation as mere mental consent has led in some places to the idea that professed Christians, who are obviously not living godly lives, are not unbelievers but merely "carnal Christians." We have accepted the unscriptural idea that one may receive Christ

---

[2]See Gary S. Maxey and Peter Ozodo, "The Hyper Grace Challenge," *The Seduction of the Nigerian Church* (Lagos: WATS Publications, 2017), 181-198; Michael L. Brown, *Hyper-Grace: Exposing the Dangers of the Modern Grace Message* (Lake Mary, FL: Charisma House, 2014).

as Savior but never give evidence of a changed life. This is a dangerous and exceedingly false teaching. It has led to a situation where we have unrepentant fornicators, adulterers, liars, etc., who are nevertheless accepted among us as "saved" because they have prayed a prayer to accept Jesus. Theirs has been a manipulative salvation, to say the least.

We have seen that Paul's testimony of the Thessalonians was that they not only turned from their idols, but they became followers or imitators of both Jesus and Paul (verse 6: "You became imitators of us and of the Lord"). The obvious teaching here is that to be born again means to leave our lives of sin and rebellion and to start an upward journey on God's great highway of holiness. Yet in our modern churches we have a lot of falsely so-called "carnal Christians" among us who need to wake up and realize that they are not the real deal. They are relying on a bogus salvation that will not withstand the fires of God's judgment.

<u>Salvation by proxy</u>. Another common practice in our day is for preachers to put words into the mouths of their hearers and declare them born again. "Pray this prayer after me," they say. In and of itself that may not be a harmful practice, though it certainly lends itself to possible misunderstanding and abuse. The real harm comes when the preacher then says, "You have prayed the prayer, and you have said you believe, so now you are saved." This is what I call salvation by proxy salvation based on someone else's declaration. Yet the problem is that almost always that type of "salvation" is without the corresponding witness of

the Holy Spirit. Paul reminds us in Romans 8:16, that it is not the witness of another person but rather that of the Holy Spirit that marks true salvation. "The Spirit himself bears witness to our spirit that we are God's children." No one but the Holy Spirit has the authority to declare a person as born again.

The result of our modern "salvation by proxy" is that now we have thousands who say, "I prayed a prayer, and the preacher said I was saved." The serious problem is that such prayers and such belief do not necessarily mean there was any repentance (turning around), or any changed life. Our preachers today and our churches have lost the ability to urge sinners to fully repent, to fully seek the face of God, and to take the necessary time to get serious about leaving the sin business behind and to count the cost to follow Jesus. Instead, we much too often rush them through our little memorized and robotic salvation rituals. We then say a few words of assurance over them and declare them as born again.

This is not the kind of practice that will lead to strong churches. It is to be feared that 95% or more of such people will go home with unresolved problems of sin and rebellion still disturbing their lives. It is no wonder that today's Church is much too often anemic and unable to serve as salt and light in a needy nation!

<u>Salvation by osmosis</u>. There are a growing and remarkable number of people populating our churches, who have made their way into "salvation" but not by way of radical humbling, repentance, and restitution. Rather, they have

opted into the church by means of family relationships or by joining the church and gradually taking on the language, color, dress or demeanor of those around them. They have blended into the church background, but they have never been crucified with Christ and have never become true saints of God. That is why we can say that the salvation of such people has been not by transformation but by osmosis gradually soaking up what is around them. To them the experience of Paul on the road to Damascus looks like fiction, because there is nothing in their own experience about a radical departure from their former life. This is not the religion of the New Testament!

RESTORING OUR FOCUS

More than ever before we need in our churches a return to rugged teaching and preaching on repentance, confession and restitution. During the course of the great revivals of history, the reality of the backslidden condition of the Church has always become clear. It has become plain that the Church has become filled with dead people, backslidden people, or people who never slid forward but who nevertheless claim to be a part of the Church. The great need for thorough repentance has always been made clear in the heat of revival. Therefore, more than ever before, we need to be clear in our teaching and preaching about the way of salvation.

We must learn to be more careful in our churches about how we present the way of salvation to those who are not born again. I am aware that some have complained about the alleged shallowness of asking people to "accept Jesus," or to "receive Jesus into your heart." It is true that such terminology has been abused, largely because it is taken in a shallow sense. The crux of salvation is to yield ourselves to God, and not to make a shallow "decision for Jesus." We must be honest to note that not all of these terms are necessarily contrary to scripture. However, the potential problem is that the way we present them can be counter-productive.

Paul wrote to the Ephesians, for example, and said, "I pray that according to the wealth of his glory he may grant you to be strengthened with power through his Spirit in the inner person, *that Christ may dwell in your hearts through faith*" (Eph. 3:16-17). We can see from this passage that the concept of inviting Christ into our hearts by faith or accepting him into our hearts by faith is consistent with scriptural expression. However, when such terminology completely bypasses preaching or teaching about humbling of our hearts, sorrow for sin, sincere repentance and thorough confession it becomes potentially misleading and dangerous.

The presentation of the gospel as seen in Paul's writings is clear. He describes the new birth as passing from darkness to light: "For you were at one time darkness, but now you are light in the Lord" (Eph. 5:8); "He delivered us from the power of darkness and transferred us to the kingdom of the Son he loves, in whom we have redemption, the forgiveness of sins" (Col. 1:13-14). He also describes it as passing from death to life: "But God, being rich in mercy, because of his great love with which he loved us, even though we were dead in transgressions, made us alive together with Christ" (Eph. 2:4-5).

I fear that in our vain and misguided attempts to make the gospel palatable to lost sinners, we have often betrayed some of the most fundamental teaching of the scriptures. That is why we must resolve to reverse course and truly put first things first.

The foundation of Christian life must begin with sound conversion, and that is precisely what Paul is celebrating in 1 Thessalonians 1. The old life of sin and disobedience must end and we must celebrate new life in Christ. We must rejoin Jesus of Nazareth as he expressed it to Nicodemus, in the simplest terms possible, "You must be born again!" (John 3:7). There can be no question that the Thessalonians knew exactly what that meant. They were the real deal. And they are a pattern for us even in our own day.

> **The primary concern the Thessalonians have conveyed to Paul is about their unanswered questions concerning end times and the Second Coming of Jesus. Yet we can now begin to see that Paul's personal concern is not nearly as much about when and how the Second Coming would take place. Rather, his concern is whether he and the Thessalonians will be found "blameless before our God and Father" in that day.**

1 THESSALONIANS 2-3:
UNFINISHED BUSINESS

After talking exclusively about the Thessalonians in Chapter One, Paul turns around in Chapter Two to talk mostly about himself. We know from Paul's letters that he was under frequent attacks from false teachers. There were people who tried repeatedly to discredit both his person and his teaching. The authenticity of his apostleship was called into question. He was accused of being a greedy mercenary. He was slandered as a wicked and profane man who sought to win over others through flattery. As a result, Paul found it necessary to remind his spiritual children of the authenticity of his divine calling and true apostleship.

PAUL'S FATHERLY TRANSPARENCY

In the twenty verses of Chapter Two, Paul reasserts his love, pride and joy over the Thessalonians, yet his primary objective is to defend himself against the false accusations that have been leveled against him. He takes seriously his mentoring role. He therefore believes that those who are out to maliciously undermine his authority are seriously jeopardizing his fatherly influence over these new believers. He assures the Thessalonians that he came to them without seeking personal benefits but rather in the midst of intense suffering.

He reminds them that he had come to them from a lot of pain and anguish in Philippi (vv. 1-6). Without putting any kind of unnecessary burden on the Thessalonians, he worked day and night among them and did so in transparent integrity, relating to them as a loving mother or father. Furthermore, he carefully assures them that he is not doing his work because of greed for money (vv. 712).

Paul's seriousness about the message of holiness, and the fact that he understood holiness to be a matter not just of theology but also of practical living, is clearly borne out in verse 10. It is typical of what we see elsewhere in Paul's thinking and writing. "You are witnesses, and so is God, as to how holy and righteous and blameless our conduct was toward you who believe." WOW! How many of our pastors and leaders in today's Church can honestly and without fear of contradiction say that kind of thing to their congregation?

It is important to understand that this is not vain or fleshly boasting. Rather, Paul is giving clear testimony to the genuineness of his convictions about holy living, and his awareness that as a leader he has a primary obligation to lead by example and practice what he preaches.

In verses 13-16 Paul once again refers to the exemplary lives of the Thessalonians themselves, and how they persevered in the midst of suffering, by continuing to imitate both God himself and Paul as their father and mentor. He concludes Chapter Two with words of further commendation for these people, in whom he has already expressed great pride and joy.

PAUL'S YEARNING TO VISIT THESSALONICA

Chapter Three opens with Paul showing just how deeply interested he is in providing further spiritual and pastoral guidance to the new Thessalonian converts. He notes that his concern for their welfare is great enough that he decided to forego his personal dependence on his faithful assistant Timothy, in order to send him back to them to provide strength and encouragement (3:1). That Timothy not only made the trip back to Thessalonica, but also that he has returned with the good news that their faith remains strong in spite of their persecution is a significant relief to the apostle (3:6-9).

However, in spite of Timothy's encouraging news about the spiritual life of the Thessalonians, it is clear that Paul is still quite eager to get back to Thessalonica. He lets them know that this is for two reasons. First, he clearly remains concerned that their persecution for the faith might cause them to falter or fail. Paul himself is well accustomed to suffering for his faith in Jesus Christ. Yet knows these Thessalonians are young converts, who might easily become discouraged to the point of failure.

AN UNEXPECTED CONCERN

The second reason for his desire to return to these people is at the heart of what Paul writes in verses 10-13. It is here Paul says something rather unexpected. With the return of Timothy, bringing Paul the good news that the Thessalonians are holding fast in their faith, it would be easy for us to assume that Paul would drop his idea of going there in person. For one thing, travel in those days was far more daunting than it is today. One of the doubtless reasons Paul kept himself surrounded by much younger men like Timothy was quite likely because of the stresses of travel. However, Paul is if anything more eager than ever to personally get back to Thessalonica. He now reveals to them a rather unexpected concern that is troubling his mind and heart.

Paul confesses in verses 10 and 11,

> We pray earnestly night and day to see you in person and make up what may be lacking in your faith. Now may God our Father himself and our Lord Jesus direct our way to you.

He is letting them know that there is something about them that is serious enough that it is causing him to lose sleep at night he is praying for them "night and day." And what exactly is his concern? He explains that he is desperate to "supply what is lacking" in their faith.

What in the world is happening here? Up to this point there is not a single hint that there is anything lacking in these wonderful people. However, what Paul could see was that despite their unmistakable spiritual life, there was major *unfinished business* in their lives. He further believes that they are now ready to take another step forward in their faith journey. It is clear that these people are not like those who spring up quickly and then just as quickly wither away. The thorns have not served to choke them; rather they are filled with a deeper resolve than ever. Therefore, Paul knows that they are ripe and ready to go *deeper* with God.

Paul gives a further hint at what he is talking about in 3:12-13.

> And may the Lord cause you to increase and abound in love for one another and for all, just as we do for you, *so that your hearts are strengthened in holiness* to be blameless before our God and Father at the coming of our Lord Jesus with all his saints.

These Thessalonians were quite unlike the foolish Galatians, who thought they had to "help" God through their own meritorious works. They are not trying to pursue some kind of works-righteousness. Yet Paul sees that they definitely need to go deeper with God. They need to experience a deeper and stronger sanctification. And, now, Paul wants to help them know a deeper level of faith than they have ever yet exercised, and to achieve a deeper level of cleansing than they have known. Paul is urging them on to a deeper experience of love, and he assures them that it is what God has done in his own life for them (v. 12).

Verse 13 ties together the two broad themes of this letter the Second Coming of Jesus and the need for deeper sanctification. The primary concern the Thessalonians have conveyed to Paul is about their unanswered questions concerning end times and the Second Coming of Jesus. Yet we can now begin to see that Paul's personal concern is not nearly as much about when and how the Second Coming would take place. Rather, his concern is whether he and the Thessalonians will be found "blameless before our God and Father" in that day.

Paul could have chosen to just give them an academic lecture on the Second Coming, including all of the events leading up to it, and how various types of people would relate to it. We can see from 1 Thessalonians 4:13–5:11, and again in 2 Thessalonians 2:1-16, that their end-time questions were heavily engaging their minds. They wanted Paul to jump into their debates and solve their nagging worries. But, as always, Paul is first and foremost not a lecturer of theology but a pastor and a mentor. His primary concern is spiritual. He knows there is a fundamental underlying issue that is far more important. The biggest issue is not about exactly when and how Jesus will return, but rather about their own spiritual preparedness for that great event. Paul is baring his heart to them now in this letter because he knows he will not see them anytime soon, and he wants them to take the next vital step in their spiritual journey. That is what lies most heavily on his heart.

This is an extremely relevant lesson for our own day. No less than in the First Century, holiness and blamelessness before God should be far more important to us today than questions about when and how Jesus will come again. We know he has promised to come. All true believers should love the thought of the appearing of Christ (2 Tim. 4:8). We must never cease to preach and teach the truth of the Second Coming. We must not be lulled to sleep by those who say we should eat, drink and be merry because Jesus is not coming soon. Yet the far more important question for all of us is whether we have gone on to the deeper cleansing and deeper sanctification that will make us eminently ready to meet Jesus at his return, whether that happens today or 100 years from now (v. 13).

OUR UNIVERSAL NEED

We can see that despite his great testimonies about the spiritual life of the Thessalonians, Paul was concerned that there was something *lacking* in their faith. We will see in Chapter Four and Chapter Five of 1 Thessalonians more clarification about the deep concern Paul is feeling. But at this point we can already say that Paul is talking about something that is not peculiar to the Thessalonians alone. Rather, there is something quite universal about it. There is a universal Christian experience that involves the discovery of unfinished business in the lives of new believers that are eager for more of God. What each of us does about the unfinished business is of huge consequence in our lives.

What we are seeing is that sanctification in the life of a believer is not a once-and-for-all, momentary happening.

It is true, as I noted in Chapter One, that Paul believed and taught that at the point of conversion or regeneration we experience the "washing of regeneration" (1 Corinthians 6:11). That washing can be properly called sanctification. At the inception of the new birth experience, all Christians are "sanctified in Christ" (1 Cor. 1:2), and thereby rightfully become "saints." Yet the work of sanctification continues thereafter in the life of obedient believers. There is an ongoing rejection of all that is unlike Christ and an ongoing receiving of more of the spirit and nature of Christ.

In order for this further sanctification to take place, it is necessary for believers to give full cooperation to the Holy Spirit. One of the most important ministries of the Holy Spirit is to convince believers of their deeper need.[3] Sooner or later, as eager and obedient believers continue to walk in the light of the Holy Spirit, they will discover this deeper need. It is frequently quite difficult for new believers, who are caught up in the excitement of new life in Christ, to imagine that they have any kind of serious spiritual deficiency. To them it may easily appear that they have all they need and that their lives are now oriented 100% for God. The newness of pardon and liberty in Christ is usually exciting. Usually there is not even a remote thought of anything contrary to God.

Yet sooner or later, we come back down to earth, so to speak. We now begin to realize that there is in fact

---

[3]This is an important part of my message in my earlier book about holiness, Gary S. Maxey, *The Highway of Holiness,* Chapter Four (Lagos: WATS Publications, 2018), 74-76.

something *lacking* in our faith. Without losing our commitment to Christ, we nevertheless begin to detect within ourselves telltale signs of conflict. We know what it is to have temptations coming at us from outside, often prompted by the devil or his dark angels. Yet, eventually, we see that there are conflicts going on deep within our hearts that are not from Satan himself but from what James refers to as the double mind.

James, in his characteristically blunt manner, describes a type of believer who is "a double-minded individual, unstable in all his ways" (James 1:8). What he is talking about is a believer who is going strong for Jesus but who is also carrying in his most inner being a contrary spirit, trying to pull him in the opposite direction. Jesus is all about genuine love, for example, but inside there is a spirit of envy and jealousy fighting against that love. Jesus is all about forgiveness and peace, but inside there is a warring spirit of unforgiveness and anger. Jesus is all about surrender and self-denial, but inside there is a struggle for independence and self-centeredness. Jesus is all about humility and meekness, but inside there is a spirit of pride seeking dominance.

That is the double-mindedness to which James refers. I dare say that virtually any believer who has walked with God for some time, in obedience and a desire for more of God, knows what these struggles are about. They have discovered their own double-mindedness. James says the result is that they are unstable in all their ways.

That is exactly what Paul is concerned about with these great Thessalonian believers. They are genuine believers. They know God. They are moving forward. But Paul says, "There is something lacking." Paul knows that if the instability they are confronting is not seriously addressed, there will be certain trouble and even possible disastrous defeat down the road.

As Paul moves forward into Chapters 4 and 5 he spells out even more clearly what he is talking about. He points to some of the potential telltale signs of their spiritual lack. And, most importantly, he gives them a clear picture of God's solution and how they can experience the deeper sanctification that will give them the greatest possible confidence that they will be ready to meet Jesus in the air when he returns.

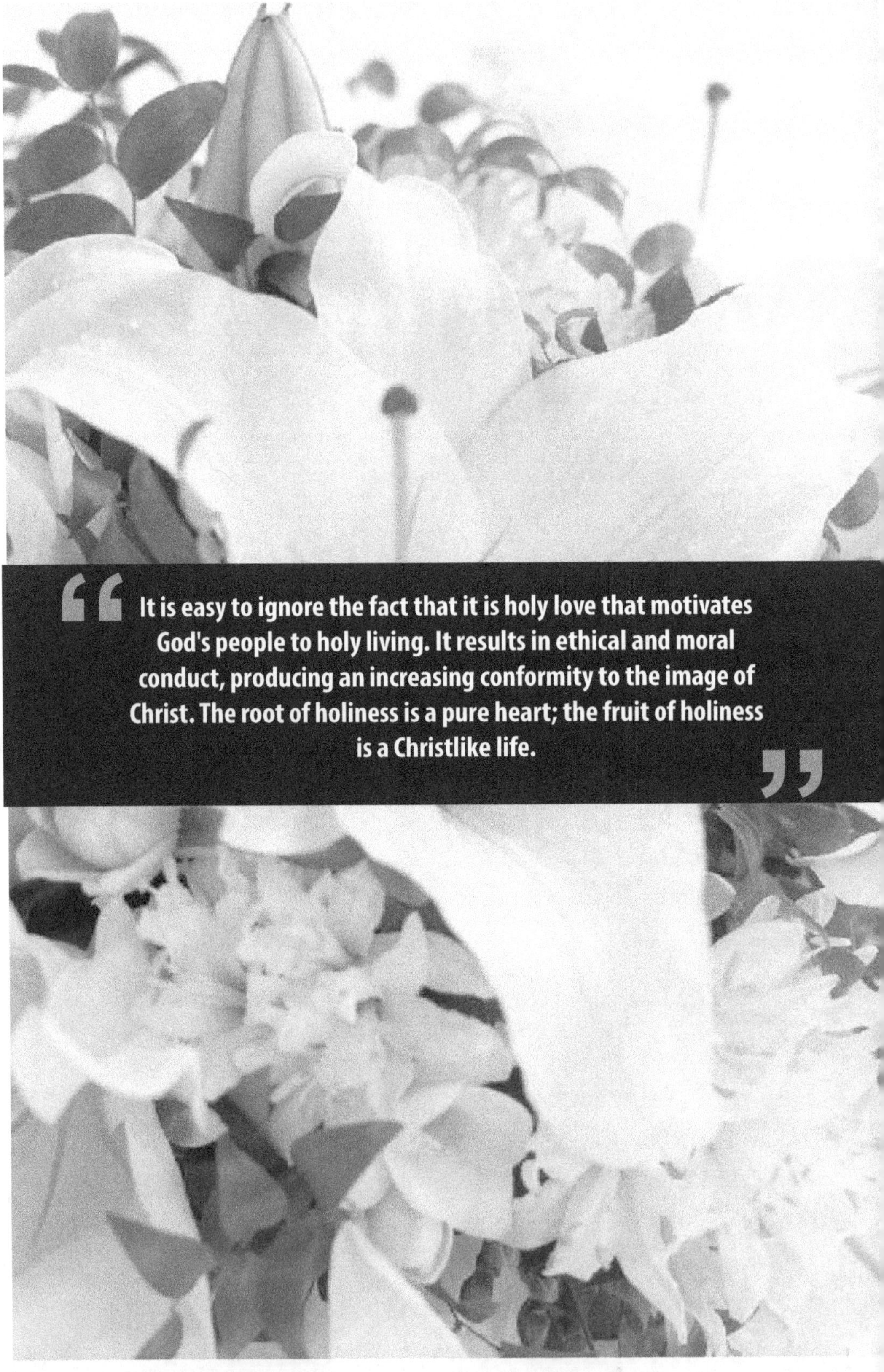

" It is easy to ignore the fact that it is holy love that motivates God's people to holy living. It results in ethical and moral conduct, producing an increasing conformity to the image of Christ. The root of holiness is a pure heart; the fruit of holiness is a Christlike life. "

Chapter Five

I THESSALONIANS 4-5:
THE NEED FOR A DEEPER SANCTIFICATION

As we move from Chapter Three to Chapter Four in 1 Thessalonians, we may find ourselves still asking, what exactly is this unfinished business about which Paul is writing? What exactly was their lacking in faith to which Paul refers? What is it they still need? Paul identifies the answer clearly in Chapter 4. In one simple word, it is *sanctification*, or being made holy. He says to them, "For this is God's will, your sanctification" (4:3 ESV).

We have seen that Paul has already spoken to them about sanctification and the need to live holy lives. He even affirms that that is what they have been doing. They are definitely traveling on God's great Highway of Holiness, just like all other truly born-again believers who continue to walk in the light. Yet he is saying there is a way this holiness must now *increase*.

> Finally then, brothers and sisters, we ask you and urge you in the Lord Jesus, that as you received instruction from us about how you must live and please God (as you are in fact living) *that you do so more and more.* For you know what commands we gave you through the Lord Jesus. (1 Thes. 4:1-2)

There is an important caution to be noted. Paul is not pressing them toward a sanctification based on their own works. There are preachers in our own day who can clearly describe the ideal Christian life of holiness, but who do not always give clear answers as to how it is attained. It is one thing to hear God say, "Be holy," but it is another thing altogether to see how that holiness is attainable. Unfortunately, we are often left with the impression that holiness has a lot to do with just trying a lot harder. For many people, the deeper Christian life means to become exceptionally serious about how we live. We appear to be preaching sanctification by doing or not doing certain things and by being highly disciplined.

I do not want to suggest that discipline is bad. To the contrary, discipline is important. In fact, the deeper sanctification of believers is not possible without serious discipline. But the pathway to that sanctification is not through simply trying harder. Rather, it is through faith, as is so true also with our new birth. It reminds us of Paul's lament in Romans 9:32, over the failure of Israel in the Old Testament to attain to the righteousness of God. His testimony was that "they pursued it not by faith but (as if it were possible) by works."

Deeper sanctification is not for the elite few, who go the extra mile in personal habits and discipline. Paul condemns that approach. It is what he calls living by the "flesh" rather than by the Holy Spirit (e.g., Romans 8:1f). It is why we say emphatically that sanctification is not about leaving off things such as the viewing of television, the wearing of jewelry and makeup and putting on things such as extra long dresses, and a joyless and somber face. At least some of those things might be acceptable in and of themselves, yet in a million years if they are done in our own strength and through the force of our own desires will never produce even a single ounce of Bible holiness. It is easy to ignore the fact that it is holy love that motivates God's people to holy living. It results in ethical and moral conduct, producing an increasing conformity to the image of Christ. The root of holiness is a pure heart; the fruit of holiness is a Christlike life (see 1 Tim. 1:5).

Paul pinpoints the pathway to this deeper sanctification not as some kind of higher discipline but as a question of *faith*. Paul has already told them in the previous chapter (1 Thes. 3:10) that there is something lacking *in their faith*, and not in their personal discipline. So we can be assured that he is not writing to them merely to tell them to get more serious about their personal discipline as a pathway to deeper sanctification, or their adherence to a long list of regulations. He knows that exhorting people about what they should do, apart from the indwelling power of the Holy Spirit, only leads people to despair.

We should recall that the legalistic solution to greater godliness (following more human regulations and depending on the strength of personal fortitude) was what made Paul so deeply angry with the Judaizers who were lambasting and confusing the Galatian church. He asked those Galatians some important rhetorical questions:

> Did you receive the Spirit by doing the works of the law or by believing what you heard? Are you so foolish? Although you began with the Spirit, are you now trying to finish by human effort? (Gal. 3:2-3)

Paul is confirming the fact that we do not get saved by faith and then move on to sanctification by works. Rather, it is by faith all the way through. We are born again by faith, and we get into this deeper sanctification also by faith. That's why Paul says to the Galatians, "live by the Spirit and you will not carry out the desires of the flesh" (Gal. 5:16).

What that means in practical terms today is that we must stop thinking about sanctification as living a strict rules-keeping life, or getting really serious in our commitments, or making sure we are more "holy" in our actions than others around us. That approach not only inevitably leads to pride and personal frustration, but it also has led multitudes who are looking on to turn their back on the very idea of holiness or sanctification.

We should note that this "works trap" I am talking about here was not just a problem with the Galatians. Paul also wrote to the Colossians warning them of that same legalism bondage:

> If you have died with Christ to the elemental spirits of the world, why do you submit to them as though you

lived in the world? "Do not handle! Do not taste! Do not touch!" These are all destined to perish with use, founded as they are on human commands and teachings. (Col. 2:20-22)

Clearly, if God is going to take the Thessalonians to the deeper sanctification that they (and we ourselves) definitely need, it is not going to be by their good works. We can neither attain nor live out the deeper life of holiness that God has for us, through our own strength or through our own spiritual engineering. Rather, in response to our own obedience and faith it will come about through a deeper illumination, a deeper conviction, a deeper cleansing and a deeper inhabitation by the Holy Spirit. It is a divine operation all the way through, and it is attained by obedience and faith.

Another mistake that some make at this point is to believe that this deeper work of the Holy Spirit is a simple matter of "tarrying." They build their understanding on the experience of the early apostles in the Upper Room, leading up to the spiritual birthday of the Church at Pentecost. Jesus told those early believers not to scatter prematurely after his ascension, but rather to tarry in Jerusalem. They obeyed, and then met together for ten days before they experienced the outpouring of the Holy Spirit that marked the beginning of the most remarkable church growth movement in history.

Based on that narrative, the teaching of some is that we, too, must engage in lengthy prayers as we wait for some kind of explosion of Holy Spirit power. Often there is a sense of passivity about it, as people tarry in expectation of an emotional visitation of God. Sometimes there is a strong focus on emotional singing and emotional praying, and a belief that it will culminate with a manifestation involving a great motional outburst. Yet we must be candid to note that there is nothing in Paul's writing to the Thessalonians which points in that direction. He does not tell the Thessalonians that they should passively tarry for an outpouring of the Holy Spirit.

UNDERLYING ISSUES

What we can see in Chapter Four is that this matter of the deeper sanctification of the Thessalonian believers was connected with their need for a deeper cleansing in specific areas of their lives. If we bear in mind that Paul writes as a faithful pastor and also a loving father to these believers, we can see several issues that he calls to their attention. He also knows that it will require the work of the Holy Spirit to bring them to a point of clear conviction for their need.[4]

Paul begins to express some of his concerns in verses 3-5.

> For this is the will of God, your sanctification: that you abstain from sexual immorality; that each one of you know how to control his own body in holiness and honor, not in the passion of lust like the Gentiles who do not know God (ESV).

---

[4]In this section I am especially indebted to John Oswalt for his observations about 1 Thessalonians 4 and 5. See John N. Oswalt, *Called to be Holy: A Biblical Perspective* (Anderson, IN: Francis Asbury Press, 1999), 151-159.

If we study all of Paul's thirteen letters we can see that dozens of times he refers to Christian believers, right from the time of their conversion, as "saints," or "holy ones." Paul believed strongly that sanctification begins at the moment we surrender our lives to Jesus Christ and begin to walk in newness of life. But now he calls for these "saintly" Thessalonians to experience a deeper sanctification (v. 3). There is something potentially confusing here. They are already God's holy people, yet he is calling them to sanctification. The answer to the potential confusion is that Paul is talking about is a *deeper sanctification* than they have previously known.

This is not the only place in Paul's writings that he calls God's holy people to a deeper level of holiness. For example, he assured Timothy of the importance of God's holy believers cleansing themselves (2 Tim. 2:10). He also appealed to the already-sanctified Corinthians, "Therefore, since we have these promises, dear friends, let us cleanse ourselves from everything that could defile the body and the spirit, and thus accomplish holiness out of reverence for God" (2 Cor. 7:1). In all of these cases it is clear that Paul is not talking about initial sanctification, but about going on to a deeper sanctification. God desires to give us a deeper cleansing than we experienced when we first embraced the gospel and experienced the washing of regeneration.

In verse 3 Paul specifically ties his appeal for this deeper sanctification to their need to keep away from *sexual immorality*. He is not writing to them because they have once again fallen back into their former sinful life of sexual immorality. There is no such suggestion here of that. On that issue we should recall that in Chapter One he commended them as model believers. Rather, he is saying that having been forgiven of their former immoral living and having been delivered from a life of willful sexual immorality, they now need to have the *root* of lustfulness cleansed from their hearts. He knows quite well that to fail to go on to this deeper cleansing could lead to eventual backsliding and returning to their former wicked lifestyle.

I have already pointed out the fact that First Century Thessalonica, like most other large cities in the Roman Empire, was known for its sexual immorality. We know that the same is true even today in most of the large cities around the world. It is not a secret that one of the primary areas where Satan seeks to defeat humanity is through our God-created sexuality. Sex is a gift from God, but it is also a major arena where Satan attempts to distract, defeat and finally destroy as many of us as he can.

Clearly, Satan has a deep hatred for human sexuality. I suspect that the reason for that hatred is because Satan knows that it is through sexual relations that more human beings in the image of God come into this world. Samuel L. Brengle, one of my favorite holiness writers, expresses it this way:

> The instinct and power of reproduction is the noblest physical gift God has bestowed upon man; it makes man a partner with God in the creation of the race, and therefore the prostitution of that noble instinct

and power is the vilest and worst of all crimes, and has brought into the world more sorrow, shame, disease, ruin, and woe than probably all other crimes combined.[5]

Though God had delivered the Thessalonian believers from their former lives of sexual immorality, Paul is now appealing to the Thessalonians to allow God to deal with the spirit of lustfulness that remains within them as a part of their double-mindedness. He wants to see a holy and pure God endue them with Holy Spirit power to control their sexuality more than ever before. On the other hand, if they fail to go on to deeper cleansing and deeper empowerment in this area they are in clear spiritual jeopardy.

This message is no doubt as important, or perhaps even more important, to people living in the Twenty-First Century than it was in Paul's day. Especially because of the worldwide web and because of the pervasive influence and impact of the international news media, sexual morality is under attack twenty-four hours of every day in our modern world. Virtually everyone, including teenagers, and even pre-teens, are bombarded with explicit temptations to lustfulness more than ever before in history. Satan is having a field day over this issue, all around the globe. Marriages are bombarded relentlessly. Premarital sex is at an all-time high in many of our societies.

---

[5]Samuel Brengle, "Sins Against Chastity," *Love-Slaves, The Collected Works of S. L. Brengle,* [Kindle, loc 8507]

We are painfully aware that homosexuality is becoming a threat even in countries where it is still generally considered a taboo. The formerly unthinkable idea of homosexual "marriage" is now front and center in many modern societies. Nudity and promiscuity are increasingly depicted in a positive light and regarded as normal not just by what we pick up internationally but by Nollywood and the social media within our own African countries. We cannot deny that we live in an increasingly dangerous age, when it comes to the issue of maintaining biblical sexual values. It is absolutely morally and spiritually fatal to ignore this unwelcome reality.

This makes it all the more important as believers, who have fled from the rebellion of our former lives, that we *go on* to experience the deeper sanctification to which Paul is calling the Thessalonians. We must not ignore the fact that the inherited sin principle within us has the capacity to lure us back into our old ways. What Paul is praying for is that the Thessalonians will experience a deeper cleansing that will ensure their freedom from any inner tendency that would lead them back into their old life. We do well to consider the implications in our own lives!

A second specific area of needed deeper cleansing and sanctification that Paul points out, in verses 9 and 10, concerns their *love for others*.

> Now on the topic of brotherly love you have no need for anyone to write you, for you yourselves are taught by God to love one another. And indeed you are practicing it toward all the brothers and sisters in all of

Macedonia. But we urge you, brothers and sisters, to do so more and more, . . .

It is helpful to remember that the crux of the need for deeper sanctification in the life of believers has to do primarily with being freed from the sinful human tendency toward self-centeredness. Even with our initial surrender to Christ at the time of our new birth there yet remains in the heart of every believer a tendency to favor and pamper self. It is as though both Christ and self are sitting on the throne of our hearts. On one hand we feel and believe we are all for Jesus. Yet on the other hand there is a constant struggle or self-centeredness that surfaces and threatens the supremacy of Jesus. As a result, we still hang on to our "right to ourselves," as Oswald Chambers likes to describe it. This is why Paul says to the Galatians, who were facing this same need, "Those who are Christ's have crucified the flesh with its passions and desires" (Gal. 5:24).[6]

It is only when self is decisively crucified through this deeper sanctification that it is now possible to have the kind of pure brotherly love that is urgently needed in the Church. Only through the faithfulness of the Holy Spirit, in illuminating our hearts, can we see this need. As believers, we must earnestly open our hearts and pray David's prayer in Psalm 139, "Search me, O God." When

---

[6]Oswald Chambers, *My Utmost for His Highest, An Updated Edition in Today's Language,* Edited by James Reimann (Oswald Chambers Publication Association, 1992), See his readings for March 21, September 24, September 28, October 5 and December 9. August 14. Chambers says, "It is not a question of giving up sin, but of giving up my right to myself, my natural independence, and my self-will."

that happens it is not uncommon for the Holy Spirit to reveal to earnest believers the impediments that prevent us from having and displaying untarnished love for others.

We must allow the Holy Spirit to deal ruthlessly with our selfishness. He must show us the spirit of envy and jealousy that can so quickly spoil the purity of Christian love. It is amazing that envy and jealousy can thrive even in the hearts of people who love one another, but such is the subtleness of the fleshly mind. And only with the deep cleansing of the Holy Spirit can love flourish in its purest form.

The Holy Spirit can also enable us to see our carelessness in yielding to temptations to gossip and evil surmising that hinder or at times even stop the flow of love within our circle of fellowship. There is little doubt that all of these things were flourishing in the lives of the Thessalonians, and it was with divine wisdom that Paul therefore urged them on to a deeper love-life.

Jesus had pointed out in the Sermon on the Mount the ideal of Christian love to which God calls every believer. He said, "So then, be perfect [in love], as your heavenly Father is perfect" (Matt. 5:48). Many people read those words out of context and imagine that Jesus was calling people either to an impossible standard or to something that will be attainable only in a future age. To the contrary, Jesus was calling all of his disciples to a standard of love that is available to all of us here and now, provided we will go on to this deeper sanctification in our lives.

If we look closely, we can see a third area of specific need for deeper cleansing revealed in the next chapter, 1 Thessalonians 5:12-15. Here he is talking about *our attitude toward those around us.*

> Now we ask you, brothers and sisters, to acknowledge those who labor among you and preside over you in the Lord and admonish you, and to esteem them most highly in love because of their work. Be at peace among yourselves. And we urge you, brothers and sisters, admonish the undisciplined, comfort the discouraged, help the weak, be patient toward all. See that no one pays back evil for evil to anyone, but always pursue what is good for one another and for all.

If we read between the lines here, we see Paul addressing the need for the crucifying of the fleshly tendencies that again and again have destroyed good churches from the inside. People who have not experienced the deeper cleansing of the Holy Spirit often find it difficult to submit to those in authority over them. They chafe under the authority of others. Furthermore, if they happen to be in leadership, they can find it difficult to exercise the necessary patience to work with those under them who are weak, or discouraged or undisciplined.

It is easy in our modern churches, even among good-hearted believers, to give in to a spirit of backbiting, quarreling, and returning evil for evil. When the human heart has never experienced the deeper probing of the Holy Spirit to reveal the need for deeper cleansing, our churches will always run the risk of decay and destruction from within. Paul's burden is real, and it is as though he understood not only what was going on at Thessalonica but that he could look ahead to our own day and give us the same warning.

SETTLING DISTRACTING QUESTIONS

Paul knows what the solution is to all of these problems. That is why he is writing to the Thessalonians with such fervor. Yet as we come to the passage in 1 Thessalonians 4:135:11 we see Paul momentarily divert his focus back to the questions that were plaguing the minds of the Thessalonians and that had prompted their enquires to him. He wanted deeply to get across to them their need for this deeper sanctification, but he knew also that they were seriously concerned about their questions regarding the return of Christ. They were questions that had most likely caused confusion and probably even disturbing quarrels among them. Though Paul surely knew these questions were of a secondary nature, like a wise father he takes time to address them before issuing his final appeal and prayer for them.

There is much to learn from Paul's comments about end-time conditions and events. One of the first things that is obvious is that Paul does not believe we should choose between being people with heads or people with hearts. What I mean by that is that the Thessalonians had some intriguing theological questions that they were debating and Paul did not ignore those questions. Yet on the other hand he knew there were strong issues of heart-holiness that also needed to be addressed and about which apparently the Thessalonians were unaware.

That is the way it should work at any good seminary or Bible college. Those who look at seminary training primarily as the attainment of a theological degree, with proper national and international accreditation, run the danger of elevating the head above the heart. I will not go so far as someone I know who has suggested that PhD might stand for "permanent head damage," but I have to admit that in some cases he may be right. However, that is only when we forget to cultivate the heart along with the head.

Bible colleges and seminaries that keep these two things properly balanced (the head and heart) are rare. A long time ago we discovered at West Africa Theological Seminary, that our deepest and most honest assessment of this dichotomy is that both academics and spiritual life are of nearly equal importance. We are convicted that there should be a primary position for the cultivation of the heart what we normally call spiritual formation but that theological learning or the academic side must also be of the highest order. After all, Jesus ran his own three-year Bible College in Palestine many years ago, and while he did not hand out diplomas or degrees at the end, eleven of his twelve students turned the world upside down within thirty years after their graduation.

So Paul takes time to answer the theological questions, which in this case centered on the Second Coming of Jesus. As with Oswalt, he knew that "right living rests upon right doctrine, and right doctrine is not right unless it results in right living."[7] Even as he seeks to answer their questions, he continues to stress from several angles the necessity for believers to go about their lives in such a way that they will be ready for the return of Christ at any moment. As I have heard my own preacher-father say probably a dozen times, "Let me live my life so that I am ready for Jesus to return at any moment, but to plan my work as though he might not return for the next 100 years."

PAUL'S POWERFUL CULMINATING PRAYER

The climax of Paul's message to the Thessalonians is clearly the prayer we see in 1 Thessalonians 5:23-24. It is the highlight of his entire letter. It is in a real sense the continuation of what he said toward the end of Chapter Three, where he bared his heart to the Thessalonians about their need to go on to a deeper sanctification. In other words, everything from the beginning of Chapter Four up through 5:22 is parenthetical and preparatory for this most fervent prayer.

> Now may the God of peace himself make you completely holy and may your spirit and soul and body be kept entirely blameless at the coming of our Lord Jesus Christ. He who calls you is trustworthy, and he will in fact do this.

This is strong language. He speaks in superlative form. The prayer is not just that God should make the Thessalonians

---

[7] Oswalt, *Op cit*, 157.

holy but that he should make them *completely* holy, or *entirely* holy. The Greek word *oloteleis* is a superlative form of the word *telos*, or "perfect." That is why I have chosen to refer to what Paul is driving after as *deeper* sanctification.

Paul believes this deeper sanctification will deeply affect every area of their being spirit and soul and body. It will purify and empower them in such a way that they will be kept blameless right down to the coming of Jesus. It is therefore a sanctification that will deal with all their needs for inner purification. It will deliver them from all their fleshly tendencies toward lustfulness, self-centeredness, backbiting, etc.

In verse 24 Paul rushes on to remind his spiritual children that this sanctification is not something of our own making. Its perfection in their lives does not depend on their own works. As with all of the operations of the Holy Spirit in our lives, it is received not by our works but by faith. The reason we know we can be God's wholly sanctified people is because God himself is the one who wills it. And when we receive it by faith, we can be further assured that God will perform the work in us. That was Paul's assurance to his Thessalonian children.

Oswald Chambers looks at this great work of the Holy Spirit in our deeper sanctification and asks a poignant question:

> Am I fully prepared to allow God to grip me by His power and do a work in me that is truly worthy of Himself? Sanctification is not my idea of what I want

God to do for mesanctification is God's idea of what He wants to do for me. But He has to get me into the state of mind and spirit where I will allow Him to sanctify me completely, whatever the cost (see 1 Thessalonians 5:23-24).[8]

With this prayer, Paul has delivered his heart to his Thessalonian children. He is proud of them, for all that God has done in their lives. He has seen them not only excel in their lives but also become examples and evangels to other around them, at home and in surrounding areas. Now he has delivered his heart to them fully, with his conviction that they must embrace the deeper work of the Holy Spirit in their lives, to be all that God wants them to be. He has faithfully delivered his heart once more.

---

[8]Oswald Chambers, *Op cit*, Reading for August 14.

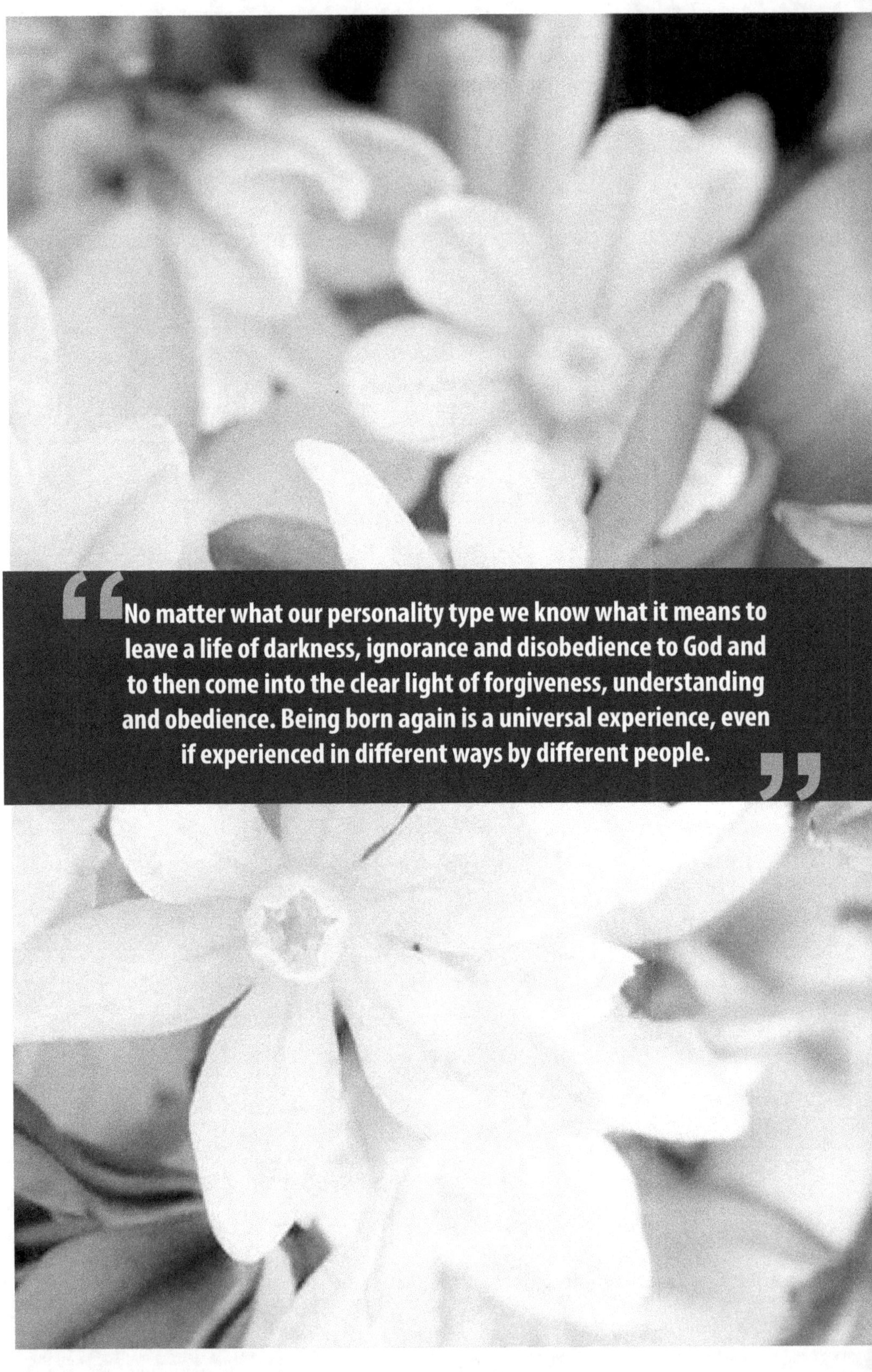
No matter what our personality type we know what it means to leave a life of darkness, ignorance and disobedience to God and to then come into the clear light of forgiveness, understanding and obedience. Being born again is a universal experience, even if experienced in different ways by different people.

CHAPTER SIX

IT IS FOR US ALL TODAY

How shall we respond to Paul's burden in this letter? It was written nearly 2,000 years ago, to a small group of people in Thessalonica. Yet because it is the inspired Word of God, the full audience and readership is fantastically larger. It is the message of God to Christians of all ages. It is a clear call to holiness. It is an undeniable message to all believers in all ages that we must go on to the deeper sanctification that is the birthright of every believer. This Thessalonian Road is of practical importance for all of us.

Why is this important? My fear is that a large percentage of those who are born again in our own day, never go on to the fullness of Christian maturity that is theirs for the asking. Instead, they struggle with spiritually up-and-down living and never scale the spiritual heights to which God calls them. They never understand what is hindering them from going deeper with God.

Sadly, many of our people never hear clear teaching or preaching on what is involved in traveling what I am calling the Thessalonian Road. As a result, they live and die without discovering the incredible spiritual treasures and blessings that are theirs.

POVERTY IN THE MIDST OF RICHES

A good illustration of what I am talking about is the story of the Yates Pool, in western Texas. When I was nine years old, my pastor-father moved our family from the arid plains of western Nebraska to the even drier sagebrush-and-sand town of Odessa, Texas. Odessa was a booming oil town in those days, sixty-some years ago. In my mind, I can still smell the odor of the oilfields and feel the sharp sting of wild sandstorms on my face as I rode my bicycle to school. We lived not far away from the famous Yates Pool.

The Yates Pool is one of the largest natural oil reservoirs in the United States. It was named after Ira and Ann Yates. They were sheep ranchers who 100 years ago settled west of the Pecos River in Texas, in what for many years was considered almost worthless land. Yates had started out in his early adulthood as a cowboy, and then for several years tried his hand as a grocer. Eventually, against the better advice of almost all his friends, he sold his grocery business to purchase about 20,000 acres of land.

Yates began to try to make a go of it as a sheep rancher. For several years, he struggled just to survive. It seemed apparent at several points his friends had been right in telling him that the purchase of such worthless land was the most foolish mistake he had ever made. For several years he wasn't able to make enough on his ranching operation to pay the principal and interest on the land mortgage. He was in danger of losing the whole thing.

But then, in the mid-1920s, while still struggling to make a profit, on a hunch Ira Yates approached the Transcontinental Oil Company and convinced them to drill for oil on his ranch, despite its unlikely location. He knew that US laws made him the owner not just of his 20,000 acres, but all of the potential mineral rights under the surface. However, although plenty of oil had been found in West Texas, the experts did not believe that there was any oil west of the Pecos River. Yet Yates was a persuasive man, and Ohio Oil (which later became Marathon Oil) also joined in the venture. Eventually they came up with three completely dry holes. It appeared to be a lost cause.

However, Yates somehow convinced them to try the drilling of a fourth hole. That is how on October 28, 1926, at 1,115 feet below the surface, they struck a huge high-pressure oil reservoir. It instantly created a "gusher," shooting oil high into the air. Over the coming days, the fresh oil filled nearby canyons that had to be dammed up as huge holding ponds.

The result was that Ira and Ann Yates became instant multimillionaires, earning even in those far-away days as high as $180,000 in a single day. That first well came in at 80,000 barrels a day, and many subsequent wells were more than twice as large. As of today, the Yates Pool has produced more than one billion barrels of oil, making it one of the largest in the US. According to the experts, there are still at least one billion estimated barrels of recoverable oil remaining, with 360 wells currently pumping oil.

Here's the point: Ira and Ann Yates owned all of that oil right from the day he sold his grocery business and bought those 20,000 acres. The day he purchased the land, he received the oil and mineral rights. Yet, for years he stared apparent economic failure square in the eyes. He was in effect a multimillionaire living in threatening poverty. The problem, of course, was that he didn't know the oil was there even though he owned it.

I believe, that in the same manner many Christians live in a state of relative spiritual weakness and even threatening poverty that is totally unnecessary. On a daily basis they face struggles with some of the problems about which Paul wrote to the Thessalonians believers. They are God's children, without a doubt, but they are living without enjoying the fullness of the benefits for which Christ died. "Therefore, to sanctify the people by his own blood, Jesus also suffered outside the camp" (Heb. 13:12). The point is, that we do not have to live in relative spiritual poverty when the fullest riches of Christ are so abundantly available.

Paul's solution is a simple one, and it is the same that is echoed by the writer to the Hebrews: "Therefore, leaving the discussion of the elementary *principles* of Christ, let us go on to perfection, not laying again the foundation of repentance from dead works and of faith toward God" (Heb. 6:1). Both Paul and the writer to the Hebrews urge us to go on. There is no place for complacency, or for stopping and resting on our oars. We must go on.

NO TWO JOURNEYS ARE IDENTICAL

We need to continually reiterate the fact that each of us has our own journey to take with God. Trying to make identical comparisons with others can be a difficult and at times a confusing matter. Psychologists have tried to help us by telling us that there are at least four fundamental personality types. Some of us are more phlegmatic (relaxed and peaceful); others are more sanguine (optimistic, active and social). The choleric type (short-tempered, fast or irritable) may tend to have more emotional religious experiences. On the other hand, the melancholic type (analytical, wise and quiet) may be rather unemotional. God loves all of us equally, and the Holy Spirit deals with each of us according to our own temperament.

Underneath all of it, however, there are common issues. First, no matter what our personality type we know what it means to leave a life of darkness, ignorance and disobedience to God and to then come into the clear light of forgiveness, understanding and obedience. Being born again is a universal experience, even if experienced in different ways by different people.

Second, every one of us can and should know what it is to move forward in Christian obedience, and to eventually discover the struggle in our inner being between our deep desire for God and the temptations and unChristlike tendencies of our fleshly nature. If we are alert spiritually, we will sooner or later enter that battle zone and we will be faced by the choice to either succumb to those fleshly desires and begin to slide backwards or to move forward toward more light, deeper consecration and deeper cleansing. No two journeys will be identical, but the pathway is the common one that millions of those before us have successfully taken.

OBEDIENCE IS MANDATORY

I have reminded my readers elsewhere of John Oswalt's simple dictum in his masterful book, *Called to be Holy*. "The way to God is by grace; the walk with God is by obedience."[9] As each of us walks forward with God in obedience, keeping our hearts open to the deeper dealings of the Holy Spirit, we will inevitably find ourselves traveling on this Thessalonian Road to a deeper death to self, a deeper consecration, a deeper cleansing, and a deeper sanctification.

The simple question we ask in this concluding chapter is, How do we do that? Knowing that God wants us to be all that he ever made us to be, and that there are a multitude of hindrances that can keep us from that worthy goal, how do we move forward? I am urging us to consider seven golden steps that we can and should take to make that a reality. I am

---

[9]John Oswalt, *Op cit*, 104.

not talking about a one-two-three magical formula, but rather about common elements in a forward journey. We are like Ira and Ann Yates, with the availability of incredible riches lying at hand. Because of the sacrifice of Christ, those riches are now rightfully ours. We are fully entitled to this blood-bought heritage, and it is truly for all of us right here and right now.

STEP ONE: I Must be Born Again

If there is any lesson from I Thessalonians 1 that we can learn, it is that before we can talk about Christian maturity or moving forward in our spiritual lives we must be sure we are born again. There is nothing more fundamental than this first step. To talk about going on to a deeper sanctification when we are uncertain about the genuineness of our conversion is a waste of time and energies and can only lead to confusion. We must not assume that church membership or spiritual vocabulary or seminary degrees are the same thing as the "narrow gate" about which Jesus spoke to Nicodemus.

Jesus warned that even the performing of miracles in his name was not a proof of salvation. Likewise, the fact that I display apparent spiritual gifts or do great deeds of service does not automatically make me a child of God. The fact that I believe the Bible and can quote scripture and teach theology is not evidence of personal salvation. James said, "You believe that God is one; well and good. Even the demons believe thatand tremble with fear" (James 2:19).

If we find ourselves in confusion on this issue, my strong advice is that we get down on our knees and begin to humble ourselves in acknowledgement of any areas of rebellion against God about which we are aware. True salvation involves humbling, repentance and turning from our wicked ways. As we do that, God will for Christ's sake hear our prayer and forgive us.

STEP TWO: Hungering After Righteousness

Once we are sure of our new birth, the next step is for us to begin to seek for more of God. The first thing a newborn baby does, under normal circumstances, is to start looking for the mother's breast. Instinctively, babies feel hunger and thirst. And so it is with those who are normal children of God. They have a natural hunger and thirst after righteousness. They want more of God. They desire to get closer to God. They seek after the fellowship of the believers. They want to feast on the word of God. They cherish the place of prayer.

Many of our churches do not adequately encourage this hunger and thirst, but as believers we can cultivate it and encourage it ourselves. As Leonard Ravenhill says,

> This is the hour when we are asked over and over again, "Is everybody happy?" God's purpose for us is not happiness, but holiness! Soberness has given way to silliness, even though Paul in writing to Titus warns both young and old, "Be sober."[10]

---

[10]Leonard Ravenhill, *Why Revival Tarries*, Kindle, loc 1013.

What we can easily miss is that God's purpose for us is not necessarily happiness, but holiness. The pathway to holiness involves the cultivating of a true hunger and thirst for righteousness. Jesus has assured us, "Blessed are they that hunger and thirst after righteousness, for they shall be filled" (Matt. 5:6). Our daily prayer therefore should always be, "O God, give me more of yourself, and show me how I can have more of your holiness and righteousness in my life." Robert Murray M'Cheyne prayed this way: "Lord, make me as holy as a pardoned sinner can be."[11]

STEP THREE: Humbling Myself Before God

Spiritual progress in our lives must be measured by our willingness to continually humble ourselves in the sight of both God and man. God must remain at the center. In order for that to happen we must have the spirit of John the Baptist: "He must become more important while I become less important" (John 3:30).

It is regrettable that many times in our contemporary churches there is an air of self-importance that is contrary to the spirit of humility. It is closely related to what I call *cheap triumphalism*. We are taught to see ourselves as perpetual winners and as constant wielders of spiritual powers. It is not improper for us to exercise spiritual authority as God's children. However, that authority must constantly be balanced by our willingness to recognize God as the only true sovereign before whom we bow in humbleness and obedience. We must be cautious to not divert attention from God himself and put the attention

---

[11] https://www.mcheyne.info/quotes.php. Accessed 8 October 2018.

solely on ourselves. We must be willing to *"become less important,"* and not give way to the temptations to pride.

When Jesus gave out his own formula for spiritual success and growth, in the Sermon on the Mount, he gave as the first beatitude the familiar words, "Blessed are the poor in spirit" (Matt. 5:3; Luke 6:20). This is a clear call to recognize our spiritual poverty without God. We think less of ourselves and more of God. We remember the words of Christ that "apart from me you can accomplish nothing" (John 15:5). It is when we adopt this attitude that we can become most open to hearing what the Holy Spirit wants to reveal about the depths of our own heart. Without the spirit of humility we will remain deaf to the still small voice of God that is so critical to our onward journey.

STEP FOUR: Welcoming Holy Spirit Illumination

One of the most important ministries of the Holy Spirit is the illumination of the human heart. Jesus told his disciples that when the Holy Spirit would fully come into the world, after his own ascension to the Father, "He will convict the world of sin, and of righteousness, and of judgment" (John 16:8). The conviction of the Holy Spirit extends not only to those who do not know God but also to the hearts and lives of those who are born again. He is convicting them not of the kind of rebellion that they once exhibited when they were far away from God, but rather of the *inner sin nature* that still resides within them. It is of extreme importance that believers attune their hearts and their spiritual eyes to see what the Holy Spirit wants to show them.

This illumination of the Holy Spirit is precisely what David longed for when he cried out, "Search me, O God, and know my heart; try me, and know my anxieties; and see if *there is any* wicked way in me, and lead me in the way everlasting" (Psalm 139:23-24). He apparently would have agreed with Jeremiah's later assessment that "The heart is deceitful" (Jer. 17:9), which applies not only to the heart of sinful rebels but also to the divided and fleshly heart of believers. It takes the penetrating light of the Holy Spirit to reveal to us the unwelcome truth about the unChristlike characteristics within us. It is when we welcome the Holy Spirit's illumination that we can begin to move toward the deeper cleansing that God wants to give us.

As a young believer, I was appalled to discover a spirit of jealousy within my heart, even toward my best friend. That spirit of jealously was so persistent that it rose to the point that I had thoughts of wishing he were dead. It came out of an ugly and unChristlike tendency within me. I loathed it when I saw it. It was not the work of Satan, but of my own divided heart. I could not deny it or wish it away. David's prayer was not for deliverance from demonic powers, but for God to reveal "any wicked way in me." That is the important work of the Holy Spirit. We must realize also that it will only come and continue as we boldly welcome it. "Search me, O God!" That must be our prayer.

As a child, I sometimes entertained myself by going to the family garden looking for a large rock I could suddenly pick up, or turn over. I wanted to see how many and what kind of bugs and worms and other creatures were there, and then to watch them quickly scurry out of sight when the light of the mid-day sun was suddenly turned on them. I had no idea of what was under the rocks, until I turned them over.

That is a good metaphor for what happens when the Holy Spirit shines his searchlight on our hearts. Suddenly things are revealed that we did not know were there. The natural result is that those things try to quickly escape and move out of sight once again. The fleshly heart does not like to be exposed to God's light and will do everything possible to avoid it or to escape it. It is a painful thing.

We see our carnal anger, but we quickly excuse it and avert our attention ("That's just the way we respond in my family," or "I was fully justified in speaking as I did"). We see the lustful trend of our attention or our thinking, but we quickly excuse ourselves. Yet if we are to move higher with God and experience the deeper cleansing that he offers, we must stop long enough to take the illumination of the Holy Spirit seriously.

I thank God for the day as a young believer, that I finally got honest enough with myself to admit that I did not have a clean or undivided heart. I definitely knew I was born again. I clearly knew I was walking in obedience to God. But I finally admitted, "I know I have not experienced this deeper sanctification that Paul is talking about." That was a huge step forward toward ultimate victory and the deeper cleansing I needed.

STEP FIVE: Confessing my Deeper Need

Seeing our inner need and confessing it out to God are two different things. I can look at my inner need for a hundred years and know that it is there, and yet never find God's holy solution. If I never confess it out I am not likely to move forward. There are lots of believers who have unChristlike anger or unChristlike gossip and divisiveness in their lives and who know those things are there. Yet too many times those very people have not humbly confessed it all out to God.

The Bible takes confession seriously. "If you confess with your mouth that Jesus is Lord and believe in your heart that God raised him from the dead, you will be saved" (Rom. 10:9). It is important that we not only see and believe in our heart, but that we verbalize it in prayer. When the Apostle Paul found himself in the throes of the struggle with sin in his life, he cried out to God, "Wretched man that I am! Who will rescue me from this body of death?" (Rom. 7:24).

The sincere believer who has seen through the illumination of the Holy Spirit what he or she could not see before, and what perhaps no one else around would have seen or known about, must now deliberately confess the need to God. There is an important scriptural principle here. God does not bring us to any area of needed cleansing in our lives, without first showing us our need and without us then acknowledging that need and confessing it to him. It is when that is accomplished that true faith can be unleashed and the work of God finally accomplished in our lives.

STEP SIX: Welcoming a Deeper Consecration

It would be wrong for me to suggest that these steps are identical with everyone or that they are necessarily of equal significance in every case. The question I most frequently ask those who are seeking more of God and who are interested in this deeper sanctification in their hearts is simply, "What can you tell me about the deeper dealings of the Holy Spirit in your life?" If I cannot give an answer to that kind of question and I do not know what the Holy Spirit is dealing with about my spiritual life and progress, then perhaps I need to set aside significant time for a serious *tête-à-tête* with God.

A primary problem is just that we are *too busy* to know where we are spiritually and where we are going. Life is going on all around us, and at a high speed. That is the kind of day and age in which we live. Yet, the deeper dealings of the Holy Spirit almost always take time. Spiritual issues cannot be rushed.

For those who do take time to wait upon the Lord, and who are truly hungering and thirsting for more of God, it is common for them at some point to face the need for a deeper consecration. Every one of us must and do surrender our lives to God when we are born again. To become a child of God is to allow God to come into our lives and begin to change our priorities and take charge of our destiny. However, sooner or later we will come to a place where God demands a deeper surrender than we have known before. He will at some point seek to ask us for a total separation to himself.

Here is where we ourselves can face the kind of testing that God put Abraham through in Genesis 22, asking him to sacrifice his son of promise. To say that it can be a painful experience is no exaggeration. Having confessed our need for inner cleansing and having owned up to the root of sin in our hearts, it is now a question of whether we will put God completely ahead of everything else in our lives. We definitely handed our lives over to God when we were born again, but now God calls us to a much deeper level of surrender and consecration.

What I am talking about here is something that is 100% driven by the Holy Spirit. It is not something I do. It is not a regimen I engineer. It is not a checklist I go through. It is not something I put on my calendar. Rather, it is opening my heart to whatever the Holy Spirit is saying to me. Abraham did not decide to demonstrate his consecration to God by offering to slay Isaac. That would have been strange and would have totally lacked authenticity. Rather, he lived closely enough to God and apparently wanted to know God as deeply as possible. As a result, God himself put Abraham to the test.

The Holy Spirit is still doing that sort of thing, yet only in the lives of those who are deeply hungering and thirsting after righteousness, and who have been totally honest with God in facing their deeper needs. When that happens, the Holy Spirit will almost always bring each of us to a place of personal deeper surrender. He will test us in the area of surrendering our human relationships, as he did with Abraham. At other times, he may ask us to surrender our right to have money or material possessions of one kind or the other. And ultimately he will ask us to give up our right to ourselves, laying our most cherished plans and ambitions on his altar and watching them go up in smoke. The Holy Spirit knows what he is doing, and how to lead us through the kind of consecration that will open the door for our final spiritual triumph.

STEP SEVEN: Receiving Deeper Sanctification by Faith

None of what I have talked about here will ever have ultimate meaning and will never lead to final victory, unless faith is now kindled for heavenly fire to fall and consume the sacrifice. Do not forget that Paul told the Thessalonian believers that there was something lacking *in their faith*. He did not want them to *do* something, but to *believe God* for something. Yes, they needed to face the fact that there were areas of their lives that needed to be cleansed, as he talked to them about in Chapter Four. But when all was said and done Paul knew that every grace of God in our lives is received not by our works but by faith. "By grace are you saved through faith," and that is as true for the deeper cleansing of the Holy Spirit as it is for the new birth.

YES, IT IS FOR US ALL TODAY

Leander L. Pickett wrote a song in 1897 that for many years was a favorite at holiness camp meetings in the USA. While I do not agree 100% with Pickett's theological interpretations, I do agree wholeheartedly that God has for every hungry-hearted believer a soul-rest beyond the all-too-common struggle with the divided heart. It is not God's intention for believers to be perpetually weighed down with what James called the double mind. Rather, he wills for all of us to experience a deeper consecration, a deeper rest, and a soul satisfaction that will carry us above the storms of life and land us safely on heaven's shore.

Here is what Picket wrote:

1. Have you ever felt the power
    Of the Pentecostal fire
    Burning up all carnal nature,
    Cleansing out all base desire,
    Going through and through your spirit,
    Cleansing all its stain away?
    Oh, I'm glad, so glad to tell you
    It is for us all today.

    ❖   *Refrain:*
         It is for us all today,
         If we trust and truly pray;
         Consecrate to Christ your all,
         And upon the Savior call;
         Bless God, it is for us all today.

2. Jesus offers this blest cleansing
    Unto all His children dear,
    Fully, freely purifying,
    Banishing all doubt and fear;
    It will help you, O my brother,
    When you sing and when you pray;
    He is waiting now to give it,
    It is for us all today.

3. Some have thought they could not have it
    While they dwell on earth below,
    But in this they were mistaken,
    For the Bible tells us so;
    And the Spirit now is with us,
    He can keep us all the way;
    Then by faith why not receive it?
    It is for us all today.

4. You may now receive the Spirit
    As a sanctifying flame,
    If with all your heart you seek Him,
    Having faith in Jesus' name;
    On the cross He bought this blessing,
    He will never say us nay;
    He is waiting now to give it,
    Why not claim it, friend, today?

I believe Pickett is talking about something that is an essential part of this great Thessalonian Road. He addresses believers who know the pardoning grace of salvation. He assures them that God has a deeper cleansing for "all His children dear." And he then assures them, "It is for us all today."

Greater Things are Ahead!

It would have been a mistake for any of Paul's Thessalonian readers to believe that experiencing deeper sanctification would mark the end of their spiritual journey. He was certainly anxious for them to go on to experience the blessing he prayed over them in 1 Thessalonians 5:23-24.

Yet Paul knew that what he was praying for was ultimately their fortification and equipping for a more victorious and successful walk with God than ever before.

The same is true for all of us today. There is no saving or deeper cleansing or sanctifying moment in our lives that marks the end of our Christian pilgrimage. Rather, it is through those experiences that God offers to us a rich life of obedience and surrender that will carry us on to higher heights and deeper depths until we reach the end of our earthly journey and enter into eternal rest. Proverbs 4:18 captures the sense of that journey and paints an encouraging and promising picture: "But the path of the righteous is like the bright morning light, growing brighter and brighter until full day."

Believers who have experienced new life in Christ, and who have gone on to experience the deeper sanctification to which Paul called these Thessalonians believers have the privilege of an upward trajectory in their Christian walk that truly can and should grow brighter and brighter. It is not a life without trouble or trials or testing, but it is a life that will truly prepare us for eternity and will day after day lead us upward in that direction. We can thank God that this Thessalonian Road is our pathway to ultimate and unending blessing. Praise be to God!

Books By Gary S. Maxey

In this engaging book, *Capturing a Lost Vision: Can Nigeria's Greatest Revival Live Again?*, Dr. Maxey gives first-hand accounts of Nigeria's Civil War Revival in the 1960s and 1970s. He examines the DNA of the revival and the reasons for its decline. More importantly, he poses the vital question of whether Nigeria can once again see a revival of equal or greater impact.

"This book will re-ignite hunger for revival in the heart of the reader. . . . Dr. Maxey shares exciting perspectives to the Nigerian Civil War revival that are worth reading by all pastors, students of history and scholars. After going through this book, one must agree that there has been a dramatic shift in the Church and that there is a compelling need to return to our lost heritage. Let us humbly invite God to heal his Church." (Pastor Austen Ukachi, He's Alive Chapel, Lagos)

"As a partaker of the 70s revival, my heart was filled with emotion as I read the truth detailed in this book. Hot tears welled up in my eyes. Then a voice said to me, 'Don't cry. Greater things are ahead.' May we live to see it!" (Dr. Uzodinma Obed, Apostolic Discipleship Movement, Ibadan)

Marketing and Distribution enquiries to:

WATS Publications
West Africa Theological Seminary
36, Olukunle Akinola Street
Akinyele/WATS Bus Stop, Ipaja Ayobo Road
Lagos, Nigeria.
www.watspublications.com
sales@watspublications.com
Tel: +234 (0) 803 781 2817; +234 (0) 806 875 2197;
+ 234 (0) 802 312 2408; + 234 (0) 808 726 6310

To order copies, please contact: sales@watspublications.com
Or: ACTS bookshop and other Christian book outlets near you.

You can also order via: amazon.com (Kindle or hard copy), konga.com, okadabooks.com or watspublications.com

Recounts the exciting journey of Gary and Emma Lou Maxey and their four children from the time of their arrival in Nigeria in March 1982 to the 25th anniversary of West Africa Theological Seminary, in 2014.

"This is a fascinating book, a breath-taking account of the inspired adventure of an American family who ventured into Nigeria in 1982 with the sole aim of founding a Theological College that would address the crying need of training African Church Pastors. . . ." Rev. Prof. E. M. Uka, Prelate, Presbyterian Church of Nigeria.

"I have known Gary and Emma for the past 20 years and I am impressed, as many others, with the great work and contribution they have made in the training of Christian leadership for the Church in Nigeria and Africa. . . ." General Dr. Yakubu Gowon, GCFR (President of Nigeria, 1966-1975).

"Throughout the book I smiled, laughed, cried, rejoiced, sometimes mourned. and found myself praying, 'Do it again, God!'" - Dr. William Sillings, Chairman, Friends of WATS

Marketing and Distribution enquiries to:

WATS Publications
West Africa Theological Seminary
36, Olukunle Akinola Street
Akinyele/WATS Bus Stop, Ipaja Ayobo Road
Lagos, Nigeria.
www.watspublications.com
sales@watspublications.com
Tel: +234 (0) 803 781 2817; +234 (0) 806 875 2197;
+ 234 (0) 802 312 2408; + 234 (0) 808 726 6310

To order copies, please contact: sales@watspublications.com
Or: ACTS bookshop and other Christian book outlets near you.

You can also order via: amazon.com (Kindle or hard copy), konga.com, okadabooks.com or watspublications.com

The first book in the twelve-volume discipleship series entitled *Teach Me Your Paths*. This is superior discipleship material for Sunday schools, small groups or individual Christian growth. It is a strong starting point for anyone who seriously wishes to learn the ways of our God. You cannot understand Bible doctrine correctly without obeying God and entering into personal relationship with the Lord (John 7:17; 1 Corinthians 2:14). Therefore, experiencing one's own new life in Christ should be the beginning of proper study of Christian doctrine.

In this book, Part One (Lessons 1-8) tells about the New Birth, the wonderful experience in which a condemned and powerless sinner is made a new creature in Christ. Part Two (Lessons 9-16) tells about Sanctification, involving both crisis and process, beginning at the New Birth and continuing on throughout the life of the believer. Sanctification includes purifying of the heart and progressive transformation into the image of Christ, and it is the right and necessity of every born-again believer. Part Three (Lessons 17-24) tells about some of the issues involved in Christian growth in grace, the need of every child of God, ensuring that we persevere to the end of our race here on earth.

Subsequent volumes in this series take believers through the entire spectrum of Christian biblical and theological education to provide comprehensive discipleship training for the Church.

Marketing and Distribution enquiries to:

WATS Publications
West Africa Theological Seminary
36, Olukunle Akinola Street
Akinyele/WATS Bus Stop, Ipaja Ayobo Road
Lagos, Nigeria.
www.watspublications.com
sales@watspublications.com
Tel: +234 (0) 803 781 2817; +234 (0) 806 875 2197;
+ 234 (0) 802 312 2408; + 234 (0) 808 726 6310

To order copies, please contact: sales@watspublications.com
Or: ACTS bookshop and other Christian book outlets near you.

You can also order via: amazon.com (Kindle or hard copy), konga.com, okadabooks.com or watspublications.com

This book is a daring and no-holds-barred description of the false teachings and dangerous trends that have sent much of the Nigerian Church off course over the past four decades. Gary Maxey is joined by Peter Ozodo in describing four major threats to Christian orthodoxy that are threatening the orthodoxy of Nigerian Christianity. The first is the unbalanced Prosperity Gospel that is shown to be an import from the scripturally unbalanced American Word of Faith movement. The second is the revival of African Traditional Religion within the Church. The third threat is a subtle redefining of Christian spirituality, moving away from sound foundations in biblical morality. The fourth threat is the contemporary Hyper Grace movement, found in the teachings of Singapore's Joseph Prince and a host of American imitators. All four of these threats have become deeply entrenched in various sectors of the Nigerian Church.

With a powerful Introduction by Gbile Akanni, this book is a must-read by every Nigerian pastor, as well as discerning lay people. Maxey and Ozodo not only point out the problems but they point to clear solutions. Their conviction is that before we can expect a national spiritual revival in Nigeria we must first see a clear reformation in which these and other errors are clearly dealt with.

Marketing and Distribution enquiries to:

WATS Publications
West Africa Theological Seminary
36, Olukunle Akinola Street
Akinyele/WATS Bus Stop, Ipaja Ayobo Road
Lagos, Nigeria.
www.watspublications.com
sales@watspublications.com
Tel: +234 (0) 803 781 2817; +234 (0) 806 875 2197;
+ 234 (0) 802 312 2408; + 234 (0) 808 726 6310

To order copies, please contact: sales@watspublications.com
Or: ACTS bookshop and other Christian book outlets near you.

You can also order via: amazon.com (Kindle or hard copy), konga.com,
okadabooks.com or watspublications.com

114

This book was originally published more than thirty years ago by Rev. I. Parker Maxey, father of Dr. Gary S. Maxey. It was reprinted several times in its original American format and widely used in Nigerian Bible colleges over the past twenty years. Now this revised and Africa-contextualized edition has been produced to continue to fill a large gap in material for pastoral training for Nigeria.

Dr. Gary S. Maxey has overseen the editing of this African edition, particularly relying on the expertise of three African pastors and trainers of pastors who had opportunities to study under the original author during his numerous visits to Nigeria in the 1990s. Dr. William Udotong (who served at WATS for over twenty years, including seven years as provost), Dr. Acha Goris (who is married to one of I. Parker Maxey's granddaughters), and Rev. John Onwuka (long-time pastor of pastors) have teamed up to make this book the best on the market for ministerial ethics and etiquette.

A Guide to Ministerial Ethics & Etiquette already has a proven track record in Nigeria. We are convinced that this new edition will go much further yet.

Marketing and Distribution enquiries to:

WATS Publications
West Africa Theological Seminary
36, Olukunle Akinola Street
Akinyele/WATS Bus Stop, Ipaja Ayobo Road
Lagos, Nigeria.
www.watspublications.com
sales@watspublications.com
Tel: +234 (0) 803 781 2817; +234 (0) 806 875 2197;
+ 234 (0) 802 312 2408; + 234 (0) 808 726 6310

To order copies, please contact: sales@watspublications.com
Or: ACTS bookshop and other Christian book outlets near you.

You can also order via: amazon.com (Kindle or hard copy), konga.com, okadabooks.com or watspublications.com

Discovering the Old Testament is the second title in the series, Teach Me Your Paths. The first title, *New Life in Christ*, has been well received, and the expectation is that the ten books that are to follow will provide a robust library for introducing the basics of Christianity especially to pastors, Sunday school teachers, small group leaders and others seeking to understand our Christian faith better.

This second book is a journey through the first part of the Bible, the Old Testament. It starts with an overview of the Bible and some general issues before plunging into the thirty-nine books that make up the Old Testament. It is a well-known fact that the Old Testament is of keen interest to Africans. In many senses they find themselves more at home with the largely rural cultures of the Old Testament than do some other cultures around the world. A grasp of the history and content of God's word as revealed in the Old Testament is very fundamental to our foundation in God's revelation. We believe the present and future strength of the African Church will be far greater if we can hold this revelation very close to our hearts.

Marketing and Distribution enquiries to:

WATS Publications
West Africa Theological Seminary
36, Olukunle Akinola Street
Akinyele/WATS Bus Stop, Ipaja Ayobo Road
Lagos, Nigeria.
www.watspublications.com
sales@watspublications.com
Tel: +234 (0) 803 781 2817; +234 (0) 806 875 2197;
+ 234 (0) 802 312 2408; + 234 (0) 808 726 6310

To order copies, please contact: sales@watspublications.com
Or: ACTS bookshop and other Christian book outlets near you.

You can also order via: amazon.com (Kindle or hard copy), konga.com, okadabooks.com or watspublications.com

Confessions of a Grateful Pilgrim: Reflections @ 70, is the spiritual autobiography of Dr. Gary S. Maxey. In an unusually candid summary of his spiritual odyssey, he takes us all the way from his misunderstanding and rejection of God in his early childhood to his present activities as a pastor, seminary founder and writer. Confessions are certainly there, but also many reasons why he is today a grateful pilgrim with high hope for heavenly rewards.

Dr. Maxey describes how he came into a dynamic walk with God at age seventeen, including his personal discovery of the meaning of holiness. He also tells candidly recounts his lengthy battle with the return of pornographic addiction that had marked his childhood, and how it was eventually overcome. With similar candor he tells how after nearly thirty years of peaceful and productive marriage he faced a storm of marital stress and failure that lasted for several years before it was happily resolved.

This is a story of hope for anyone facing the common struggles of living out the Christian life in the modern world.

Marketing and Distribution enquiries to:

WATS Publications
West Africa Theological Seminary
36, Olukunle Akinola Street
Akinyele/WATS Bus Stop, Ipaja Ayobo Road
Lagos, Nigeria.
www.watspublications.com
Sales@watspublications.com
Tel: +234 (0) 803 781 2817; +234 (0) 806 875 2197;
+ 234 (0) 802 312 2408; + 234 (0) 808 726 6310

To order copies, please contact: sales@watspublications.com
Or: ACTS bookshop and other Christian book outlets near you.

You can also order via: amazon.com (Kindle or hard copy), konga.com, okadabooks.com or watspublications.com

The two-fold objective of this book is to show a clear picture of what a holy woman or man should look like and to describe the pathway for its attainment. The Highway of Holiness is metaphorical for the life of holiness that starts at the point of the New Birth and progresses throughout our lifetimes. Scripturally, all believers are saints, or holy ones, yet there is also discernible progress along the way. The author uses 2 Thessalonians 2:13, which describes our salvation to be "through the sanctification of the Holy Spirit" to talk about the operations of the Holy Spirit in illumination, separation, purification and inhabitation. In doing so, he builds on several decades of ministry in Nigeria both as a teacher and pastor.

Marketing and Distribution enquiries to:

WATS Publications
West Africa Theological Seminary
36, Olukunle Akinola Street
Akinyele/WATS Bus Stop, Ipaja Ayobo Road
Lagos, Nigeria.
www.watspublications.com
sales@watspublications.com
Tel: +234 (0) 803 781 2817; +234 (0) 806 875 2197;
+ 234 (0) 802 312 2408; + 234 (0) 808 726 6310

To order copies, please contact: sales@watspublications.com
Or: ACTS bookshop and other Christian book outlets near you.

You can also order via: amazon.com (Kindle or hard copy),
konga.com, okadabooks.com or watspublications.com

A sound grasp of the background and contents of the New Testament is imperative for any serious following of Jesus Christ. In the Old Testament we find answers to some of the most basic questions of life, including who God is, how the world was created, how sin entered the world, and how God chose to create men and women to walk with him in a covenant relationship. Yet is only in the New Testament that we get the full revelation of Jesus Christ, the Son of God sent into the world to seek and save lost humanity (Luke 19:10). In this fourth book in the Teach Me Your Paths series, we follow up on Book Two (Discovering the Old Testament) by looking at the twenty-seven books of the New Testament, understanding their background, authorship and content. This is excellent material for individual and small-group study, enabling us to better understand God's word written for all times and all people.

Marketing and Distribution enquiries to:

WATS Publications
West Africa Theological Seminary
36, Olukunle Akinola Street
Akinyele/WATS Bus Stop, Ipaja Ayobo Road
Lagos, Nigeria.
www.watspublications.com
sales@watspublications.com
Tel: +234 (0) 803 781 2817; +234 (0) 806 875 2197;
+ 234 (0) 802 312 2408; + 234 (0) 808 726 6310

To order copies, please contact: sales@watspublications.com
Or: ACTS bookshop and other Christian book outlets near you.

You can also order via: amazon.com (Kindle or hard copy), konga.com, okadabooks.com or watspublications.com